*Praise for*

# Adrian Rice

"[*Impediments*] is a book in plain language about plain people. It shares their suspicion of excessive speech—of ornamentation, rhetoric, floweriness of feeling or surface ... [it] seems, sadly and genuinely, to soul-search on behalf of its community and therefore do it honour."
   —**Ruth Padel**, author of *Emerald*

"The poems of *The Mason's Tongue* are brave children of an imagination rich with the tradition of radical dissent. Bright and plain-spoken, they must be seen and heard."
   —**Ian Duhig**, author of *The Blind Roadmaker*

"[*Hickory Haiku* is] a jewel of a book. Whenever I pick it up I find new treasures and I simply read them again and again. The poems have a feeling of two worlds—Hickory now, Ireland then. The book has a beautiful intensity, beautifully controlled by form and intellectual and emotional precision."
   —**Brendan Kennelly**, author of *The Essential Brendan Kennelly: Selected Poems*

"Along with the poetry comes a growing awareness of the 'independent airs' of radical Belfast, of the great dissenting tradition of the past, of an integrationist stance. Birds flying in and out of *The Clock Flower* poems—blackbirds, sparrows, hawks, jays—put us in mind of John Hewitt's lines about staking his future on 'birds flying in and out of the schoolroom window.' Hewitt, and beyond him the nineteenth-century Dr. William Drennan (subject of Rice's MPhil thesis), are exemplars for this poet. But Rice's voice is distinctively his own: forthright, colloquial, wry and persuasive."
   —**Patricia Craig**, *Times Literary Supplement*

"Following in the footsteps of what was once mass immigration from Ulster to the Carolinas, Northern Irish poet Adrian Rice has become a modern land breaker of poetic territories. In his new volume, *Hickory Station*, there are poems of Northern Ireland memories and others of Appalachia and the Low Country. Rice knows how to bear simple and eloquent witness to family life, the reckonings of self, and to distant and adopted homelands. Like many before him, Rice cannot forget the fields and woods outside the porch, the animals that make up the world without us. His poems are concise, poignant, and lyrical. *Hickory Station* is a warm-hearted, beautifully crafted, tour de force."
　　—**Jefferson Holdridge**, Director of Wake Forest University Press, author of *The Poetry of Paul Muldoon*

"Adrian Rice's poems expose us as the elegant animals that we are. His facile and unique control of the language can remind you of countrymen Ciaran Carson and the late great Seamus Heaney, especially when he hunkers down in the slow shadows of the trees in Western North Carolina, or in the 'real electric life' of the imagination's countryside to contemplate the violent upheavals of the Natural World. His description of a mother slowly drawing the breath of her husband from the balloons left over after a birthday party tragedy will stop your own breath. His examinations of American life with his poet wife and wee son are streaked with love and optimism. Rice uses silence like a painter uses negative space, reminding us that no matter where we go, we enter the new country with the old one still strapped on our back."
　　—**Keith Flynn**, editor of *The Asheville Poetry Review*, author of *Colony Collapse Disorder*

The Strange Estate

Also by Adrian Rice

POETRY
*Muck Island*
*Impediments*
*The Mason's Tongue*
*Hickory Haiku*
*The Clock Flower*
*Hickory Station*

NONFICTION
*The Tin God*

AS EDITOR
*Signals*
*Life of the Lough*
*Sea & Shore*
*Around the Lough*
*A Conversation Piece: Poetry and Art*
    (edited with Angela Reid)
*Lough Views*
*Exploring the Lough: Creative Activities*
    *for the Primary School Classroom*
    (edited with Molly Freeman)
*Insights*
*Shore Lines*

# The Strange Estate

New & Selected Poems
1986 – 2017

Adrian Rice

Press 53
Winston-Salem

Press 53, LLC
PO Box 30314
Winston-Salem, NC 27130

First Edition

Cover design and interior layout by Kevin Morgan Watson

Cover photograph, "John Keats in Valle Crucis 2," Copyright © 1979 by John Rosenthal, used by permission of the artist.
www.johnrosenthal.com

Back cover image
Copyright © 2012 by Ross Wilson,
used by permission of the artist.
www.rosswilsonartist.com

Author photograph by Jon Eckard, Eckard Photographic
www.eckardphotographic.com

Library of Congress Control Number
2018942974

Printed on acid-free paper
ISBN 978-1-941209-81-3 (paperback)
ISBN 978-1-941209-84-4 (hardcover)

*In memory of*
*my best friend*

Martin Andrew Beattie
(1958–2016)

*Proverbs 18:24*


*Or else perhaps*
*you lost the friend who knew you best of all?*

—*The Odyssey*, from Book 8, 'The Songs of a Poet',
trans. by Emily Wilson

## A Note from the Publisher

Since the author of this book hails from Belfast, Northern Ireland, and this book will be distributed worldwide, the editor has chosen to honor the rules of United Kingdom grammar and punctuation to preserve the voice and spirit of the author and his work. No words have been Americanized by removing a "u" from "colour" or the second "e" in "acknowledgements"; likewise, commas and periods have been left outside the quotation marks, in spite of it irritating the editor when U.S. authors do this.

# Acknowledgements

The author and publisher gratefully acknowledge the following for previous hospitality to some of these poems:

*The Asheville Poetry Review, The Belfast Anthology* (Blackstaff Press, 1999), *Bloodshot Journal of Contemporary Culture, Chapman, The Clock Flower* (Press 53, 2013), *The Echo Room, Fortnight, The Forward Book of Poetry 2001* (Forward Publishing), *FourXFour Poetry Journal, Hickory Haiku* (Finishing Line Press, 2010), *Hickory Station* (Press 53, 2015), *The Honest Ulsterman, Impediments* (Abbey Press, 1997), *Iodine Poetry Journal, The Linen Hall Review, Lines Review, Love, Remember: 40 Poems of loss, lament and hope* (Canterbury Press, 2017), *Magnetic North: The Emerging Poets* (Lagan Press, 2006), *The Mason's Tongue* (Abbey Press, 1999), *Muck Island* (Moongate Publications, 1990), *New Hibernia Review, The New Orleans Review, Poetry Congeries with John Hoppenthaler, The Poets' Republic, Poetry Ireland Review, Poetry Wales, Rhinoceros, Voices: 25 Years of The Pushkin Trust, The Ulster Anthology* (Blackstaff Press, 2007), Winston-Salem Writers' 'Poetry in Plain Sight', BBC Radio Ulster, BBC Radio 4, BBC Two Television, RTE *Arena* (with Sean Rocks), RTE Lyric FM, Ulster Television, and *Wordplay* with Jeff Davis (Asheville FM).

The author would also like to thank a posse of significant encouragers and helpers along the way: Sacha Abercorn (The Duchess of Abercorn), Nathalie Anderson, Raymond Armstrong, Martin Beattie, Michael Beattie, Gerard Beirne, Patrick Bizarro, The Captain's Bookshelf (Asheville), Jimmy Brown, George Bryan, Rick Bryant, Gerry Burns, Stephen Connolly, Patricia Craig, Paul Custer, Colin Dardis, Duane Davis, Jeff Davis, Sammy Douglas, Mike Dowdy, Ian Duhig, Keith Flynn, Maureen Gallagher, Malcolm Guite, David Hammond, Eric Hart and the Hart Square family, Lorna Hastings, Don Hawthorn, Seamus & Marie Heaney, Laura Hope-Gill, Brian Houston, Kenneth Irvine, Thomas Kabdebo, John Kelly, Kim Lenaghan, Michael Longley, Steven Lyerly (and staff of Olde Hickory Station shop), Greg McClure, John McCormick, Padraig McGuinness, Virginia McKinley (and staff of Malaprops Bookstore, Asheville), Mel McMahon, Alan Mearns, Chrisanne & Lamar Mitchell, John & Betty Orr, Philip Orr, Lois Palmer, Eve Patten & Kevin Smith, Glenn Patterson, John Pearse (ASU Bookstore), Tim Peeler, Martin Quinn, Omair Rabbani, Anne Rawson, Ian Rea, Angela Read, Jonathan K. Rice,

Matthew Rice, Jim Rogers, Mark Roper, Richard Rankin Russell, Glenn Simpson, staff of Barnes & Noble (Hickory), Mike & Sandy Stevenson, Samuel 'Sammy T' Thompson, Woodrow Trathen & Dorothy Maguire, Ross Wilson, Paul Yates, and last (but by no means least!) Kevin Morgan Watson ('The Boss') at Press 53.

My deepest thanks and love go to my amazing wife Molly (not least for channelling the cover image) and our 'wee man', Micah, for everything, especially for tholing the long porch-sits and study-stints; and to my three kids back home, Matthew, Charis and Charlotte; much love always to my mother, and brothers; and big Granda-love to my first grandchild, Ray, whose head will be well wetted in the same month as this book.

*I have always felt that a poet participates in
the management of the estate of poetry, of that
in his own language and also that of world poetry.*
—Czesław Miłosz

*There are no unsacred places;
there are only sacred places
and desecrated places.*
—Wendell Berry

*Beat your megaphones into ear trumpets.*
—William Stafford

*The poet isn't a rolling stone. He has two sacred
obligations—to leave and to return.*
—Pablo Neruda

# Contents

# Foreword

It seems hard to believe that the still-youthful Adrian Rice is already publishing a "New and Selected Poems," gathered over some thirty-one years of publishing poetry. The man and the poetry are both so vibrant, brimming with life, that it is good to know that this volume represents only a way-station, although a significant one, on a journey that we hope will last much longer. The title of this selection not only channels Czeslaw Milosz's "estate of poetry," referenced in his epigraph, but also slyly signals Rice's upbringing on the Protestant housing estate of Rathcoole, Newtownabbey, just north of Belfast, and its Loyalist ideology, depicted in poems collected here such as "The Dummy Fluter," "Sides," and "Tour of Fire." Moreover, it suggests something of his sense that the earth on which we live is a strange estate, a place from which we are estranged in certain ways. Not that Rice hasn't worked hard to make his corners of this world, ranging from Rathcoole and other parts of Northern Ireland to his current home ground of Hickory, North Carolina, where he teaches and writes, more familiar to us.

Rice also has striven hard to make and keep good friends wherever he has been *planted*—more on that verb later, which serves as the title of one of his most intriguing poems—and his dedication to this volume to his best friend Martin Beattie comes from Proverbs 18:24, translated in the King James Version as "A man that hath friends must shew himself friendly: and there is a friend that sticketh closer than a brother." Many of these poems celebrate such friendships, including ones for Beattie, or the English-language poems from *Muck Island* with their facing translations that blend Scots and Irish Gaelic, dedicated here to Aodán Mac Póilín, and Rice's lovely "Moongate Sonnets," for his departed friend Billy Montgomery.

Rice's poetry, too, instantiates a kind of loving, generous friendship with the readers of his work that mirrors the man's expansive and kind personality. Poem after poem beckon to us, inviting us in to celebrate their dance of music and words. A typical Rice poem leads us into its created world with its seeming simplicity of diction and colloquialisms, but once inside that world, we are struck with its angled and complex meanings and music and with what can only be called the persistent belief in the human *soul*.

Debts to his fellow Ulsterman Seamus Heaney and to an English poet who spent his most productive years in Belfast, Philip Larkin, are clear. Consider the Larkinesque ending of "Cardboard," a poem originally collected in *The Clock Flower* (a reference to the childhood game of blowing the seed off dandelion heads): "Face it; life's only ever really good, if it's good for you." That knowing, slightly cynical voice that enters the end of this poem recalls Larkin's, but without that poet's growing despair or eventual nihilism. And "Planted" is dedicated to Heaney and draws on, yet renovates the famous opening lines of that poet's "Bogland"—"We have no prairies / To slice a big sun at evening." Instead, Rice's poem memorably limns his new Southern home in North Carolina: "We have no porches to share a slice of melon on back home, / To sit on to watch the sun go down, least not where I come from. . . ." The music of that urban upbringing—"the squeaky brakes of passing cars" and the "sing-song goings-on of late evening's emptying bars"—has now been elided by the Carolina sounds of tree frogs, cicadas, and the "rhythmic rattling in treetops." He is careful here to balance the British word "fireflies," favored by Yankees in America, with the much more melodious Southernese for these wondrous creatures, "Lightning bugs." "Planted" still in Heaney's poetry and in his urban Belfast cityscape, Rice nonetheless puns on the historical connotations of that word in Irish history to suggest how comfortable he has become in North Carolina. The planters were largely Calvinists and other strongly Protestant settlers who were "planted" in the northern part of Ireland by the English monarchs Elizabeth and James in the early seventeenth century to break the back of the Gaelic resistance to British colonization. It's still a pejorative term in nationalist quarters of Northern Ireland, but Rice, even though identifying with "such curbside Calvinists" back in that province and their silence, reminiscent of many of Heaney's quiet craftsmen, simply admits his ancestry but concludes that he is "Happy to sit and watch as heat waves shiver into mist," an admission of his ability to escape tribal bond and bounds and let them dissolve to some degree like these Southern heat waves.

In fact, Rice is a proud dissenter, an ecumenical Protestant who takes his bearing from historic Presbyterian dissenters in the north of Ireland who emigrated from Scotland and who protested the dominance of the Church of Ireland and the penal laws levied against them and Catholics in the sixteenth and seventeenth centuries. Twentieth-century descendants of this group include the well-known poet John Hewitt, another figure of conscience for Rice and influence on his poetry. In his notes on the poems in the back of this volume, he points out that "Sometimes I Think" is "Based on a magical day in the home of another honest Ulsterman [besides Billy Montgomery], the quintessential 'dissenter'—the poet, critic and gallery man, John Hewitt (1907-1987)." Rice also terms Hewitt a "dissenter" in "Beseech" and "Freedom." Fascinatingly, Rice has discovered that he is actually descended from both Protestant and Catholic grandparents. This discovery complicates his dissenting heritage, but that complication actually heightens his own sense of contrariness. In "Related," dedicated to Brian Murphy, for instance, he ponders the Ulster dialect word "thran," which denotes one who is "Stubborn, contrary, cross-grained," much as Murphy was, and recounts his realization that he was related to this Catholic man. Another poem, "The Other Side," a clear nod to Heaney's poem of the same name, meditates upon his inherited "Catholic / granda's Mass card" and adorns his memory with three moving images—the baby St. Ambrose lying in his cradle, "dribbled with honey"; the dessert ambrosia, "nectar of the gods"; and finally "Ambrosia Creamed Rice," which he terms "the tinned working-class dish / we had to enjoy—urban / frogspawn. . . ." He revels in the juxtaposition of these ethereal and quotidian foods, decorating his grandfather's memory with them.

One of Rice's finest poems, "Breath," first collected in *Hickory Station* and nominated for a Pushcart Prize, is framed with two questions, "What is death, / but a letting go / of breath?" and "What is life, / but a drawing in / of breath?" It quietly and movingly meditates upon the death of a husband and father, one of whose last acts was to blow up balloons for a children's party, struggling "to tie all / those futtery teats." Rice's use of this Ulster dialect word to describe the balloons, themselves likened to maternal teats, plaintively sets up the conclusion of the poem, where the man's widow muses whether she should pop them all, but instead, delightfully and poignantly, gathers them up "slowly undoing / each raggedy nipple," taking "his last breaths into her mouth" with each one. Drawing on the sum of the literal last breaths of her dead husband may actually give her life as the final lines suggest.

Along with the poems of *Muck Island*, printed in 1990, other sections of the volume include *The Mason's Tongue* (1999), *The Clock Flower* (2012, revised expanded edition, 2013),

*Hickory Station* (2015), and *New Poems*. Note the significant publication gap between *Muck Island* and *The Mason's Tongue* and again between *The Mason's Tongue* and *The Clock Flower* and the current efflorescence of Rice's poetry. Without speculating on the biographical reasons for such time between volumes, suffice it to say that Rice publishes what he wants to when he wants to. Some poets fear silence; Rice seems to revel in it and not be afraid to take his time to publish quality poetry. Having said this, it is clear that his move to North Carolina in 2004 liberated his tongue and his imagination, as the recent flow of poetry, much written on the "poetry porch" of his home in Hickory, attests.

A significant strain of the most recent poems is increasingly buoyant, some of them fully enjambed, with nary an endstopped line in sight, even in their conclusion. Consider in this regard, "A Dream of Home," a sixteen-line poem composed of four quatrains featuring a moment of magical realism—a "white shirt" that "was flip-flopping / in the summer wind / when it changed into / a perfect white swan" that the speaker captures and takes home, where it perches on "the low lake of the window / -ledge and sat there staring / at the passing people." The lack of enjambment here signifies the shirt "flip-flopping" in the wind and then the swan it is changed into. By refusing to end this poem, Rice suggests how the swan is still active, staring not just at passersby but perhaps us as well! Likewise, in "Distance," a sequence of four two-line stanzas, the inability of the speaker to touch his own face "in the mirror," coupled with the lack of a period at the poem's end (or anywhere else in it), implies the distance we have from ourselves—that just as the poem is not "fixed" in place, we cannot fix finally upon our own face through touch. The last two poems of the volume, "Flame," with its shuddery, juddery flame "Against the inevitable dark," and "The Shadowed Path," with its concluding "gigantic installation / Of shadow-shapes in a gallery of air," are likewise ethereal, wavering, but nonetheless substantial, indicating how Rice trusts in the airiness of these tercet-driven poems as a substantial bulwark against the literal and figurative darkness we now find ourselves in.

It is a good thing to trust in these poems with their directness, honesty, and tenderness in a time when political and cultural discourse has been coarsened and cheapened, and when so many of us feel divided from our neighbors and colleagues over issues small and large. Another literary antecedent for Rice, the Belfast-born poet Michael Longley once said that poetry is like the pituitary gland in our bodies—tiny and unseen, but completely necessary to our health. Adrian Rice's poetry in *The Strange Estate: New and Selected Poems 1986-2017* proves poetry's health in this debased and impoverished era and thus contributes to the health of the body of this nation and others.

Richard Rankin Russell
Baylor University
Author of *Seamus Heaney: An Introduction*

# Muck Island

The following twelve poems were first published in the *Muck Island* box, accompanied by twelve images from Ulster artist Ross Wilson. As an interesting literary artefact to honour the linguistic heritage and culture of the north-eastern, County Antrim coast of Northern Ireland on which the poems were based, the poems were also translated into the particular version of Gaelic spoken by many inhabitants of the region who hailed from a Scots Gaelic background. To achieve this aim, the poems were first translated into Irish by the late Irish language activist and scholar, Aodán Mac Póilin, and then worked upon by friend and fellow Irish language speaker, Brian MacLochlainn, who also had a working knowledge of Scots Gaelic. The resultant translations are a subtle hybrid of both forms of Gaelic, which Aodán and Brian called Antrim/Irish or Antrim/Scots Gaelic. The poems and their mirror translations (collected here) are dedicated in memory of the life and work of Aodán Mac Póilin (1948-2016).

Publisher's note: For the sake of keeping the poems and translations side by side, we will begin with the first poem in this section on the left-hand page rather than the right.

# The Mason's Tongue

Although a likeable, charitable soul,
He had a less than secret tongue;
So it was removed, and entombed
A ritual distance from the shore—
Sealed dumb in the packed sand.

When a young man dug it up
(Out toiling for some bait)
It dropped from the wet spade
Onto the cool slab of strand,
And lay like an odd curl of meat.

The young man cupped it in his hands
To get a closer look,
When, stirring on his palms
And with a strangely mournful note,
It suddenly began to speak:

*Go tell all the brethren*
*There is no rest where I have gone,*
*No answer comes from Jah-Bul-On.*

Bewildered, and seized with sudden dread,
He let the tongue flop to the sand,
Then scooped it back up with his spade
And flung it out across the waves.
Yet, though hushed upon the ocean bed,
The tongue's words lapped about his head:

*Go tell all the brethren*
*There is no rest where I have gone,*
*No answer comes from Jah-Bul-On.*

# Teanga An Tsaoir

Gidh gur dhuine laghach an saor
Bha an teanga 'na bhéal ma sgaoil;
Sgathadh o ís adhlacadh
Fad na ngeasróg gnathach ón chladach—
Gaineamh dingthe thar a bailbhe.

Fleasgach óg a tháinig uirth'
(Is é ag tachailt baoite)
Thuit sí as spáid fhliuch
Ar leac lom fhuar na traigh uisgeil,
'Na ceirtlín corr feola.

Thóg an t-óglach í 'na mhám
Ach chun sealladh ní b'fhoisge,
Gun dearn sí corradh ar a bhois
Is b'ann an guth dubhach aduain,
A rinne sí bruidhinn na truaighe:

*Téigh is abair leis na bráithre*
*Nach fheil tamh ann an áit mo lonnaithe,*
*Cha dtig guth ó Jah-Bul-On.*

Le méid a iontais is a uafáis,
Thuit an teanga de phlab ar an ghaineamh,
Sgiob sé anoís lena spáid aris
Is thilg amach thar barr na dtonn í.
Ach gidh gur bhalbh ar grúnta an aigéin,
Bha focail na teangan ag slapairt m' a chloigeann:

*Téigh is abair leis na bráithre*
*Nach fheil tamh ann an áit mo lonnaithe,*
*Cha dtig guth ó Jah-Bul-On.*

# The Drowning

Seeking luck through the evening,
He spat into the torn mouth
Of the first fish pulled on board:
*Fishes' eyes have seen strange things,*
He murmured—the uneasy burden
Of a prophetic word.

With darkness came a listening wind;
The sea made mouths at us all night.
Not until the break of light
Did he come in,
Off Heddles Port—
Pockets inside out,
Mouth full of the ocean's spit.

Suppose what they say is true—
We sink beneath the sea
Lost in the flood of memory:
Then say his last journey
Was no macabre pirouette
Through the watery dark;
But that he went down serenely,
Rapt, as in a childhood zone,
In the whorling silence of a snowstorm
Under an oval dome.

# Am Bathadh

Mar comhartha áidh don choinfheasgar,
Chaith sé seile ann am béal stróicthe
A' chéad éisc dar tharraing sé ar bord:
*Is iomadh rud aduain a chonaic súile iasc,*
Ar séisean faoina anail—ualach corrach
Focal na tairngreachta.

Tháinig gaoth na h-éisteachta leis an dorchadas;
Bha craos na fairge romhainn fad na h-oidhche.
B'ann le cámhair an latha
A tháinig sé ar tír,
Foisg ar Port na hÉadala—
Pocaí tiontaithe amach,
Béal lán de sheile na fairge.

Abair gur fíor mar a deirtear—
Théid sinn faoin tonn
Ann an tuile na cuimhne:
Abair nar luascadh a' bháis
Ann an duibheagan na fairge
A thuras deiridh;
Ach gur shíothlaigh go suaimhneach,
Faoi dhraoidheacht, mar bheadh leanbh,
Ag cuaifeach tostach sneachta
Ann an ubh ghloine.

# Margaret Mitchell

*I shall go into a hare,*
*With sorrow and sigh*
*And mental torment.*

Above the hill of the man of the yellow hair,
Birds skim like stones on an ocean of air;
Clouds are thick and coloured like a bruise.
And across the sloping hilltop field,
The wind runs a light green shimmer in the grass
To where he sits and shelters by the whin bushes

... sits and broods upon the times
She'd huddled against him in that spot ...
Surely not ... was she guilty of such crimes?
What secrets had she hid from him?
When did the stated sorcery begin?

Persuaded of the magic in her rhymes,
They have stood her in the Carrig stocks
And mocked her as a crazed young witch—
Hounded like the fabled lurker in the ditch.
Yet she only used the phrases that were heard
On lips around the townlands, and beyond,
And I would laugh and scorn, in my usual way,
And she would call me rude, and swear
That I could really madden her.

But there's madder than you, my love,
Though you be as mad as a March hare:
Many who will never trace
The scars of stones upon their neck
Or feel the smack of cabbage stalks
Against a reddened face.

# Maighréad Misteall

*Rachaidh mé amach imo ghirr-fhiadh,*
*Le h-osna le mulad orm*
*Tá mo chridhe cráite, tá m'intinn trom.*

Thar cnoc an fhir fholt-bhuidhe,
Theíd éin ag sgimeadh mar bheadh clocha ar aigéan áile;
Raltachan ramhra, dath dubh-fuilteach.
Is thar an chraoisean, ni plathadh gaoithe
Loinnir uaine troimh'n fhéar ghorm
Ann am fasgadh na n-aiteann far a bhfeil sé 'na shuidhe.

Ann am fasgadh an n-aiteann ag caoidh na lathan
Ar laigh sí 'na sgiathan anns an bhad sin
… am b'urra leis gur chiontach í?
Cad iad na rúintean a choinnigh sí?
Cá fhad a rabh sí 'na du-bhandraoidh?

Nuair a thuigeadh dóibh gur dhraoidheacht a rannta,
Sheas siad go dleathach í sna ceapa Charraig
Chuaigh a mhagadh faoin chailleach chuthaigh—
Chuaigh sa tóir uirthi mar bheadh meirleach ar fhógradh inti.
Gidh nar chleacht sí ach seanfhocail a dúirt
Lucht an bhaile fearainn is ma gcuairt,
Dhéanainnse mo lachan gáire lena gnúis a dheargadh le náire
Go gcaitheadh sí drochmhúineadh leam is bheireadh leabhar
Gum b'urra leam a gríosadh as a meabhair.

Tá siad ann ar mó a mire, a ghraidh,
Más mire girr-fhiadh an Mhárta fhéin do mhiresa:
Iad siúd nach rian lena meara choidhche
Lorg na gcloch ar mhuineal;
Nach mothaigh ar an aghaidh
Liudar an ruinneal cáil.

A smurr of drifting rain
Rounded up the birds inland,
And he lifted up his hands, as if to pray,
But only breathed on them, to warm them,
Then started back for home across Drumgurland.

She lay silent in the castle hold,
As in a form, or souterrain—
Sequestered from the mind's intrigue,
The tongue's accusation,
The pishrogues of men.
*Ye yarrow, yarrow, I pull thee—*
*And under my pillow I'll put thee*
*And the first young man that speaks to me*
*Will my own true love be.*

Smúid ceobhráin anall
A ruaig ó mhuir na firéin;
Thóg sé a lámha ar nós duine ag guidhe
Ach b'ann lena anail a ghuir sé iad.
Thug sé aghaidh ar an bhaile, bealach Dhroim Dhuirling.

Laigh sí chomh ciúin ann an carcair an Chaisteil,
Is dá mbeadh sí ann an gnas girr-fheidh
Nó ann am fasgadh uaimh faoi thalamh—
Slán ar chogar ceilge,
Lucht a bhíodáin,
Pisreoga an duine.
*Athair Talmhan spíonaidh mé—*
*Cuiridh faoin chluasan ar a sín mé*
*An chéad oigfhear a chuireas foran orm*
*Mo rún-searc é ma's urra leam.*

# Rinn Seimhne Blackbird

In a Mullaghboy back garden
A blackbird lands in lush green blades,
Flirting its tail up and out
Like a satin fan waved
In the high summer heat.
With the cock of the head
From side to side,
Its bill cuts a silent yellow arc,
As the blackbird treads the ground and listens
To work his fantastical art—
A breathless sounding
Of the worm's earth-dark.

# Lon Dubh Rinn Seimhne

Ann an garradh cúil ar an Mhullach Bhán
Laighidh lon dubh go cas ar féar flúirseach frasach,
A eireball ag sméideadh suas is amach
Mar bheadh filleadh sróil ag séideadh ann an láimh mná.
Anns an tsamhradh bhruthallach.
Goic ar an cheann
O thaobh go taobh
Eistidh an lon dubh; ar an talamh ni ruideog
A ghob ag gearradh stuagh uaine
A ealáine diamhaire—
Grinnealaghadh gan tuaim
Chré-dhuibheagan na cuiteoige.

# Serpents in the Heart

When Patrick preached of redeeming blood
Rinn Seimhne spurned the druidic brood,
And turned to the adoration of God.
But cloven tongues still lingered
In neighbouring woods: and in his dreams,
The saint was strangely troubled.

Night after night the vision came,
Ulster torched by the Spirit's fire;
Each region kindled by the power
That drives the heart-blood of men:
All save the island of Rinn Seimhne, so named
Since bounded by an underground stream.

What then lurked in that place
Where Patrick had raised
The first church tower
In his Lord Christ's name?
What hidden stream of the heart
Sought to douse the Spirit's flame?

# Nathracha Nimhe an Chroidhe

Nuair a labhair Pádraig ar fhuil na fuascailte
Thug Rinn Seimhne a cúl le pór na ndraoithe,
Is thiontaigh ar adhradh Dé.
Ach sna coillte maguaird mhair fathast
An teanga liom leat: ina chodal,
Ba trom croidhe an naoimh.

Oidhche i ndiaidh oidhche a tháinig an aisling,
Cúige Uladh ar folscadh ó lochrann an spioraid;
Gach dúich adhainte ag cumhacht
Fréamhaithe ann am fuil an chroidhe:
Ach oilean Rinn Seimhne amháin, ar a scathadh
Ag scruthán faoi thalamh.

Cén rud a mhair fá scáth san áit sin
Ar thóg an Táilcheann
Clog-thaigh a chéad chille
In ainm a Thairna Chríost?
Có acu sruth fá thalamh sa chroidhe
A d'fhéach le lasair an spioraid a mhuchadh?

# The Portmuck Birdman

It was a week since they had seen him first,
from their perch on the hill above the bay.
They were watching huge and fabulous clouds
drawing shadows over the fields below,
when their eyes fixed on a solitary figure
zigzagging around the harbour

... his *Omnium Gatherum* ...

He spraightled his way across the causeway stones

Drumgurland, Dundressan, Gobbins,
Mullaghboy and Portmuck Bay,
Ballymoney and Balloo ...

Their moving moon of light
framed his ghosts of flight

While high above the birdman's head
flapped seagulls with their stammering chatter
laughing their way out over the sea

With a mouth full of pebbles
he whistled for flies

They scampered home round Skernaghan Point

The boys had a night of dreams
The birdman lay in a dreamless sleep

A fluttering of wings, no more sound than that.
O vulnerable angel, man with the cuckoo heart.

# Einfhear Phort Muc

B' ann a bha seachtain anois ona gcéad-radharc air,
ón chliath faire os cionn na baighe.
Iad ag coimhead raltachan Righ Neimhe
ag tarraingt a scáilean thar na cuibhrinn thíos,
trath, choniac siad an t-aonfhear, an t-einfhear
ag deanamh fiarlain ar chrioslach an chuain

... a *Mhala Corr* ...

Is e ag sciorr-streachailt a bhealaigh thar leaca an chlochain

Droim Dhoirling, Dun Dreasan, na Gobain,
An Mullach Buidhe, cuan Phort Muc,
Baile Muine agua Bail' Lugh ...

Tiomchuairt gheal na gealaighe
timcheall ar thaibhsean a éalaithe.

Go hard os cionn an éinfhir
faoilinn ag eiteogaigh, ag snagarsaigh
ag screadghaire thar muir.

Rinne se feadail cuileog
O bhéal lán de mhearoga.

D'imigh siad ina ruith thar rinn Sceir na habhann

Go rabh oidhche lán de thaibhreamh ag na buachaill
Is gur suan gan brionglaid codal an éinfhir.

Cleitearnach eiteog is gan de thuaim ach sin.
A aingil inbhriste, a fhir chroidhe chuaiche.

# The Corncrake

The corncrake climbed
Above the grain,
Its young left to
The reaper's blade.

He hit their soft heads
Against a stone—
To make a clean end—
As he always did.

A tidy act,
The young birds dead,
His cry of *lazy*
Damns the corncrake's head.

# An Traonach

Stréap an traonach
Ón arbhar amach,
Is d'fhág a lachtar
Ag faobhar an bhuanaidhe.

Steall sé a gcloigne
In éadan cloiche—
'Ga marbhadh go glan—
Mar ba bhéas leis.

Gníomh slachtmhar,
An lachtar marbh,
Damnuighidh sé an t-éan
Mar shlúiste gan mhath.

# Bread of Sorrows

Voices coming from the cassie:
*The room needs aired,*
*Lift the window open ... quietly.*

Every townland has one,
A muck-raking quidnunc:
She doesn't need to know
The facts, her mind swells
With a million scenarios.

A bosom-hugger,
With the bustling gait of a starling;
She will tip the wink, nudge
Knowingly ... Queen of the regular
Gabfest at the lintels of doors.

And when her day's work is done,
Settled before the blazing fire,
She'll sit there, indulging herself,
A slice of barmbrack sailing
Into her open mouth like a boat.

# Aran an Bhróin

Glórtha ag teacht ón chasaigh:
*Tá aile de dhith ar an tseomra,*
*Tóg an fhuinneog ... go ciúin.*

Tá sí ann an gach baile fearainn,
Aineolach an bhéadain:
Chan fheil uaithi an fhírinn,
A hinchinn ag at
Le mílliúm scéal scéil.

Sciathan fillte ar sheilf a brollaigh,
Chomh preab-thónach le druideog;
Caochadh súile, sonc
An eolais ... Banríon na ngeabadan
Ag féile na ndoirsean.

Agus obair an lae déanta,
Os comhair craos teine,
Suighidh si go sáthach,
Leac de bhairghean breac ag seoladh
Mar bhiodh báta ina clab mór béil.

# Going to the Stone

Heaven quietens.
Darkness is visible.
There is panic
In the flaffing of crows.
A new wind soughs,
Slumbering eyelids lift:
The stone tilts and purls
To the sea's pale steeds.

Unable to walk it had been
Carried, and chanted into place
East of the Griddle Ring.
Balanced with a priestly
Sleight of hand and mind,
It held the seat of government.
Only the wind could move it—
The wind or human guilt.

As the torque of gold
Round a judge's neck
Was felt to tighten
At truth kept dark
Under the palm's lid,
So the stone would
Cradle and rock
At the approach of the shuffling heart.

Now fallen, idle on the floor
Of the vanishing ocean—
The end of man's adultery with stone.
All around the earth groans,
Wearied of its tholing.
From heart to heart
Runs the desperate call:
*Ruat coelum*—let the heavens fall.

# Ag Dol Chun Na Creige

Thig tost ar an Neamh.
Is léir an dorchadas.
Tá baspairt ann
An leadhbairt na bhfeannog.
Caoinidh gaoth úr,
Tógthar fabhraí codalacha;
Claontar a' chréag agus tiontaithear
Chun eacha bán-ghlasa na mara.

Nuair nárbh in-siubhal i,
Chuaigh a giúlan le nuallan dona háit
Taobh thoir d'Fhainne na Gridille.
Choinnicheadh ann am meidh i
Ag cur-an-céill sagart.
Ansin a bha udaras is reacht.
Cha bhogadh ach a'ghaoth í—
An ghaoth nó éagóir daonna.

Mar a theannadh fadó
An torc óir
Ar mhuineal brethimh
Ann an láthair fíanaise
A théadh a coinneáil faoi cheilt,
Is amhlaidh a rachadh a' chréag
A luascadh agus a longadan
Ar theacht croidhe cealgaigh.

Anois díomhaoin ar ghrineall
Na mara seargaighe—
Críoch adhaltranais le cloch.
Éagaóin na maguaird cruinne,
Spíonta ag a fulaingt.
Ó chroí go croí
Ruithidh glaoigh an éadóchais:
*Ruat Coelum*—go dtuite an spéir.

# The Wing

A blush of sunset lights the path
To The Wing's at Ballywindy, Mullagdubh,
For a legendary scene in the island's history:
The undertaker's nightmare—a bodiless wake.

The Wing had disappeared without trace.
One moment the hubble-bubble of *Macbeth*;
The next, gone—
Pupils left admiring and agog.
Within his alphabet of eccentricity,
This was surely the Z.

While warm fadge and tea were passed round,
Some thought McAlshinder was spot on:
*He was a clubbable little man, all over you*
*Like a badly cut suit. Those seashell ears,*
*And that composite face—plain, ample markers*
*For anyone. It's simple—he's ghosted back under the hill.*

Yet anxious in a corner sat old McClelland,
Puzzling what The Wing had said:
*Though I love this tongue-of-land, I've made up my mind ...*
And he spoke of her swimming in
From the heart of the sea, top-half fully bared,
Cradling her catch of oysters and pearls.

*McClelland, you knew him better than anyone did.*
*What's your verdict?*
Well what could he say?
Fairies under Muldersleigh Hill seemed outlandish enough;
How then could he tell them—
*He's away with the Mermaid?*

# An Eiteog

Laigh na gréine a' deargadh a' chosain
Go taigh na h-Eiteoige, Baile Uaine, am Mullach Dubh,
Chun radhairc dúchasaigh na h-inse:
Trom-luighe fear na h-adhlactha—faire gan chorp.

D'imigh an Eiteog gan tasc ná tuairisc.
Bómaite amháin glig-glag-gliogar *Mac a' Bheatha*;
Ansin, go tobann, imithe—
Fágadh na scoláirí ina staicíní iontais.
Ann an aibitir a shaoithiúlachta,
Ba é seo go dearbh an Z.

Dáileadh amach fáidsean teth is tae,
Bha feadhainn sa chuideachta ag dol le McAlshinder:
*Fear beag laghach, thart timcheall ort*
*Mar chulaith droch-tháilliura. Na cluasa sliogain,*
*Agus aghaidh éagsamhalta—comhartha cinnte*
*Do dhuine ar bith. Gan amhras—thaibhsigh sé ar ais faoin chnoc.*

Ach bha sean McClelland buartha sa chlúdaigh,
A' meabhrughadh ar an dúirt an Eiteog:
*Gidh gur grádh liom an ros seo, tá m'intinn socair …*
Is labhair sé uirthi a' snámh isteach
Ó chroidhe na mara, lom-nocht go ruige a coim,
Oisrí agus pearlaí ar bhacan a láimhe.

*McClelland, tusa ab fhearr aithne air.*
*Caidé do bhreithúnas?*
Caidé b'urra leis radh?
B'aisteach go leor siogaí ar Maol Ard Slighe;
Caidé mar a deireadh sé—
*Leis a' Maighdean Mhara a d' éalaigh sé?*

Out and up the dark hill towards home,
With only a backward glance
At the scarf of smoke from the chimney-top,
Raising a laugh at the memory of The Wing,
Sweep's brush floundering about in the summer air—
Entirely useless:
*McClelland, if the moon had been out*
*We'd have darkened its face.*
*—Yes, Wing ... we'd have darkened its face.*

Amach is suas an dú-chnoc a' druidim ar an bhaile,
Gan ach amharc amháin siar
Ar an bhratach toite ón tsimléar,
Ag déanamh grinn ag cuimhniughadh siar ar an Eiteog,
Scuab simléir a' lonadan an aer an tsamhraidh—
Gan fheidhm gan mhath:
*McClelland, dá mbíodh an ghealach ann*
*Dhubhaimid a dreach.*
*—Seadh, a Eiteog ... dhubhaimid a dreach.*

# Stone Head, Stone Heart, Stone Hope

### I. *Hillsport, 1907*

At the east side
Of the Chapel Field
The wind stripped
The soil away,
And a skull,
Sockets fraught with earth,
Gazed across the sea.

### II. *Brown's Bay, 1956*

When the last layers were lifted,
A skeleton lay in its narrow house—
An axehead lodged between the ribs.

Wasted heart, holding such weight
Of stone, how often were you bruised
By the thud of the tongue's hammer
Long before the axehead's
Final sickening wound?

### III. *The Gobbins, 1975*

No primordial plot,
Just shot and driven
To the Gobbins cliffs.

Void of the heat
Of their loosened
Ghosts, both bodies,
Tepid to the touch,
Are left to stiffen.

Two more—long since—too much.

# Cloigeann Cloiche, Croidhe Cloiche, Dóchas Cloiche

## 1. *Port an Chnoic, 1907*

Ar an taobh thoir
De Ghort an tSéipeil
D'fheann an ghaoth
An chré gur nocht
Blaosc chloiginn;
Cuasain chlábarach a shúl
A sealladh na mara.

## II. *Cuan an Bhrúnaigh, 1956*

Nuair a scríobadh na sraitheanna deiridh,
Fuarthas cnamharlach ina leaba chúng—
Tuaigh an sas sna heasnacha.

A chroidhe seirgthe, faoina ualach
Cloiche, cá mhinic a bha tú brúite
Ag liúdar geanntair na teangan
Fada sula dtáinig
Créacht buan na tuaighe?

## III. *Na Gobain, 1975*

Cha ba chomh-chealg o chian é,
Ach loisgeadh púdair is fuadach daoine
Go beanna na nGoban.

Gan teas
A dtaibhsean saor
Ma scaoil, dha chorp
Leamhfhuara
Da gcrannughadh.

Beirt eile—o chionn fada—de bharraíocht.

# The Little Pig

Its back-end had gone
And they all nosed at it.
You nearly killed them with that stick.
Still they ate its running insides.
We pulled it across
And out of the stinking pen
For privacy to die;
Jerking it, struggling,
Into a concrete circle open to a cold sky,
And covered it,
To keep the rain off it.

I've since been told
We should have slit its throat,
Hung it up,
And that way have salvaged the meat.
I suppose we were the last romantics.
And yet, you, your boots at ten-to-two,
Hand in the air, with that inimitable stare:
*How can I go in and make*
*Beautiful pictures now?*
And we both laughed somehow.

# Am Banbh

Bha a ghiodan ite
Agus iad a' smúrthacht air.
Gé gur bheag nar mharbh tu le bata iad,
Lean siad ar cnamhadh a phutoga silte.
Shlaod sinn linn é
On chrodh bhréan
Go ruige bás priobhaideach;
A' gleacaidheacht leis, ' ga shracadh
Chuig ciorcal concréide faoi spéir fhuar,
Chaith cithdeog air
Mar fhoscadh.

Chuala me o shin
Gur chóir a scornach a ghearradh,
A chrochadh,
Leis an fheoil a shábhail.
Sinne fuidheall na romansaithe.
Tusa, is do spága ar deich go dti a dó,
Ag starrógacht ma gcuairt, lámh in airde:
*Caidé mar is urra*
*Piochtuir áille a dhéanamh anois?*
Is rinne sinne gáire, ar eigean.

*The Mason's Tongue*

# The Boyhood of Raleigh

*after Millais*

For the one boy—
A story.
For the other boy—
A different story.

# The Young Pulpiteers

I.

I used to puzzle
The gifts of coal
Crossing the threshold
On Old Year's Night,
But feel excitement
At the imagined power
Of their presence
Within my walls.

II.

Loosed to think like a man
On Ballycraigy 'coals':
Burnt willow witness,
Burgeoning black,
The bradawled pulp
Exposing to view
The icons of our minds.
Swift rubber-worked pieces;
Frozen splayed images, layered,
Lacquered and sealed in these times;
And supple, not slack.

III.

Not now vain climbing horses,
The touchwood of sense,
Hoping for chariots to take us
And doubting where they went,
But faces as flint
To the wafer of white,
Building with bands of gold
Through sirens songs of night,
Crying with that wallmaker of old—
Strengthen now our hands—
The people must be told.

# The Artist on the Eve of a Breakthrough

He is not feeling well today.
Like himself,
He feels his latest efforts on canvas are sickly.

In cut-down plastic squeezy bottles
The matted hair of each brush
Is steeping in a watery murk.
Paint clings to the edge of little tables,
Like muck skimmed off the soles of several shoes.
Here and there,
Old shirt-rags lie abandoned, stiffening with paint.
The shuttered windows
That hold out the light hold out good air.
What's left is rheumy air, laden with white spirit.
This is air you could put a match to; and it is cold.
Bags of rubbish, themselves rubbish,
Lounge around the stone floor.

Today, he is crumpled on the floor.
He is sick of his working clothes,
His old jeans like a cotton palette.
He is sick of his feeble talent.
Sick of his wanting to be elsewhere;
Of the trip-elsewhere-would-make-it-easier
To-come-back-singing-and-work-hard routine:
Verily bowelsick of such lazy evasion.

And today, of all days,
There is no solace in the wall's collage—
The amulets, inspirations, the paper prompters,
The letters of love from distant lands,
The sweet scriptural promises
Or the warning (warring) texts.

He is on his own. He is not feeling well.
Like himself,
He feels his latest efforts on canvas are sickly.

# Prize Day

*for Martin Beattie*

Take away all poppy prints
On gridded cards.

On Sunday School Sunday
Only the firsts,

With groomed teeth,
Percolate into the aisles

With any conviction—
The first being first,

Not second, or (Lord forbid)
A consolation.

Within such holy laddering,
Who or what sifts first

From consolation
In a gathered church?

# Rosebrook

*in memory of Louisa Hay*


Sky-floor is rumbling:
'God shifting His furniture'.
The heavens open.

\*


*Rosebrook* awash. As
The wind lifts, the house creaks like
An old galleon.

\*


A real ripsnorter:
A wind-scythe through tidy beds—
Funeral flowers.

\*


Miraculously,
Each Kerry Blue slate up and
Landed like a leaf.

\*


Poles standing, knock-kneed;
Lines sagging like necklaces:
Bird-bead abaci.

\*


Watching the birdies,
A soggy cat plucks netted-
Wire like a harpist.

\*


A double-yolk sun
Setting over steaming fields.
Promising weather.

# The Gift

The Protestant heart is a zoo of lust;
Its lascivious craving for conquest
Is often appeased on the Catholic rump.
Your grandmother couldn't manage her heat:
When Brown came conniving and sniffing
(Snout at the slats of the gate)
She welcomed him over the wall.

Walls are more than bricks and mortar:
She sullied all that was pure and holy;
Walls of Virtue and of Faith turned to dust.
Ill-luck from her marriage was measured for her,
And not only for her—it's your blood's legacy,
And one your expectant bride must share.
Seemingly betrothed to the selfsame surname,

Her heart's set on a gift from the Church—
Like signing the cross with the wedding ring
To wither a sty and banish a wart,
Or sexing a foetus in the slew of the ring
Dangled over the mothers' burden:
Gifts folk covet from hearth to hearth.
But no matter how connatural to the ear,

The surnames are estranged in ink.
Put simply (and without any blasphemy)
Our Lord is the Great Phonetician,
But a devil for every character of the word.
You're *Brown* with an *n*, she's *Browne* with an *e*:
Though blameless, the *e* is transparent to Heaven
And this means that no gift can be given.

The bad news will break in a rush;
Family and friends may be secretly chuffed;
But you can sweeten the sense of loss.
For her sake, suggest that Mother Nature has
Blessed her with a gift she mightn't be aware of:
A feminine thing that husbands esteem—
Like the precious gift of ............ *listening*.

# Biblical Teaching on the Devil

Sleeping on my own last night,
I was wakened by a bad dream,
So bad that I rose, fled to the bedroom
Where my wife lay sleeping,
And almost disturbed her from slumber,
For comfort, for such was my fear.

Lately, my night-time reading
Has been *Biblical Teaching on the Devil*
By William Still.

I must remember to change my night-time reading.

# Silent Argument

*for Ian Duhig*

It is not unheard of for me to entrust
My barnet to the hands of a barber
Who has years since lost his hearing.

And I have noticed how he seems more
Than a trifle nervous when his friends
Appear for a short-back-and-sides.

In ear-splitting whispers, he reveals that unless
He delivers a cut-above-the-rest, they never cease
Talking about him at the club for the deaf.

# Hold Back the Cauldrons

And as we look out
From the ramparts,
We all ask,
'Whose poem is the greatest?'

Now he's not saying this because
So-and-so's here—however,
He says,
So-and-so's is the greatest,
Packed with originality and power.

Well, since he's not saying
That yours or yours
Is less than great,
Then we all nod
And yes yes
As we gladly agree
That So-and-so's is surely
One of the greatest poems
Anyone has seen
In a long, long time.

Then while
The (wonderful! wonderful!)
Poem is read,
Some bear gentle
Smiles
And someone even
Cries.

So there it is.
Keep the gates shut.
Be vigilant.
But hold back the cauldrons
Of boiling oil.

# A Question of Guilt

I have become a pillar of darkness.
And all those who didn't ...
Who haven't ... who wouldn't ... who couldn't ...
Who can't possibly imagine how I ...
Holiday in the shade of my sin.
There they disport themselves—

Sure they can't be seen—
Like Pharisaical peacocks:
Strutting, preening, posing,
Pontificating to their heart's content.
And doing other things of which
I will not speak. Once, like them,

I would peer into the evening mirror,
Summoning up a few words and deeds
To somehow rig a manageable conscience
And a good night's sleep.
And once, I too was
Something of a sin-surgeon,

Extracting the baneful splinter
From the brazen eye. But now,
As a breaker of that which was unbroken,
I acknowledge the ugly plank—
The beam on which they see-saw
With their buoyant, sacred hearts.

'Justification by Faith? By Filth!'
So runs their festal chorus;
*Mea culpa*—once again—I suppose,
Since there remain these unsurrendering sounds
Oozing from the pool of self,
Bubbling up and babbling out

From that dismal source.
Still, one must go on—survive—
At least for certain others.
And to those who bask in my sin's shade,
I ask in deference to their apparent light:
Isn't it better to love than to be right?

# Fireguards

Changed overnight from sulky schoolkids
To tinder-hunters and rag-and-bone boys,
We slogged for weeks to build the blaze.

We bore trees like trophies from Carnmoney Hill
And hauled household junk from airless attics.
We dragged behind us the bed-wetter's mattress,

Leaving a trail like a huge slug's slither,
And palm-rolled dozens of baldy tyres
From fusty coalsheds and skittered yards.

As the bonfire rose like a wooden wigwam,
We caught the vision of a dodgy den:
We put a door in the bonfire's side

And carpeted a generous circle of grass
With scullery lino and cardboard strips
To beat the damp and the feared earwig.

Kitchen-drawer candles or hurricane lamps—
Swiped in the night from roadwork sites—
Brought to light the tell-tale litter

Of Coke cans, crisp-bags, cheap beer tins,
Nude-book pages and wet fag-ends,
Ruined Rizlas and lemonades from Yacht:

Refundable bottles religiously retrieved,
While the rest was abandoned to burn.
Although sometimes used as a lewd laboratory—

*You show me yours and I'll show you mine*—
The den was mostly a male preserve.
Whether the sun was splitting the sky

Or fog rolled in like liquid floss
Or a redbrick moon capped chimney-tops,
We sat in and looked out on painted kerbs,

Flag-draped houses and maisonettes.
Well-armed with hatchets, knives and sticks,
We guarded the bonfire from arson attacks.

# The Musicians' Union

While over the lintels on Lenaderg Terrace
The Red Hand ruffles in the tea-time breeze,
Off carpets, chairs and Chesterfield suites,
The idle are stirring from *Scene Around Six*:
For thunder is rumbling round 'Coole cul-de-sacs
And along the side entries of Executive houses;
It's shaking new windows in puttyless frames;
And startling infants, sticky with sweeties,
In their pavement prams—with two big drums
And a fleet of flutes, here comes the band.

In scruffy school uniform or funeral gear
(Fashionable fatigues for the marching season)
And Oxford brogues or black Doc Martens,
The band hits the street in a steady rhythm.
On hands and on arms, they're tattooed to a man,
With slogans and symbols for today and tomorrow
From the tattoo-template of their forefathers' skin:
There's a covenant signed with both God and Ulster;
UDA, UVF, No Surrender—and Mother,
And crimson hearts punctured by arrows.

With the bold Prince of Orange soon on the horizon,
The street is the scene for the evening drill,
But tonight the band's out on official parade.
It's canvassing time in the local election,
When bigots and brethren court doorstep opinion;
It's a chance for a band to come into its own,
So long as it carries a tuneful selection
For the voters' riposte to the Pope and the bomb—
Partisan ditties that in booths they will whistle,
Where X marks the spot and completes the charade.

# The Dummy Fluter

Huffin' and puffin', pursin' and poutin',
Struttin' his stuff at the back of the band:
'*Lips*', '*Dog Whistle*', '*Fingers*' and '*Golden*'—
The 'team' wouldn't travel without him.

No Orange credential or way with the flute
Secures him a place in this Loyalist troupe.
He could be a KAIser; a slick womaniser;
The club raconteur or the site racketeer;

Somebody's son or Somebody's brother;
Or a bit of a bastard who hammers the beer.
But when all's said and done, more often than not,
This master of no tune is basically HARD:

Hard on his Ma, hard on his Da,
Hard on his brothers and sisters and girl;
Hard on his teachers, hard on the preachers,
And hard on your face should you cross him at all.

# Sides

I. Green Light

Crouching like a fada
On top of the hill,
A dark figure
Watches for a signal.


II. Gable End

Hand on the tribal batons
And to hell with hope?
Trumpet-tongued, the grim graffito—
FUCK THE NEXT POPE

# The Big Picture

*for Raymond Armstrong*

Outside the window,
B-movie rain falls in floods.
Someone must be on my roof,
Sending those buckets down.

Other hands have the house surrounded
With cranes and booms;
The gardens tracked,
The cameras dollying along.

While the key grip corners the gaffer,
The continuity girl works
With an awkward shoe,
And the best boy does what best boys do.

I suppose they are waiting on me.
Well, they can wait.
I'm not coming out.
What's happening is happening inside.

*The Clock Flower*

# Wake Up

*in memory of Seamus Heaney*


A Carolina cardinal charging the study window
Woke me up to the Dundas winter
When a cat cried all night outside the big bay window

In the snow, black heart on cold white slab,
Coffin-lid thick. And I woke next morning
To the loss of the Russian Bard,

Disappearing just before the century closed.

And then today, in Hickory, seventeen years on,
Birds banged against the bedroom window
All morning long, while I lay with my boy

In the bed, resting our late night heads.
And I woke to the loss of the Irish Bard,
And knew well what the birds had been beating out:

Wake up!
Wake up!
Wake up!

The Poet's dead!

# The Moongate Sonnets

## Prologue: The Book of Life

He loved that moment when family members,
Long lost friends or cherished lovers,
Forgot themselves in their rush to embrace.
For him it was a foretaste of Heaven's grace.
He would hide his teary eyes by sleight-of-hand,
By channel changing and manly banter
Or by slipping to the scullery to make us supper.
He would reappear with china teacups in each hand
And create a fuss deciding which was which.
Settled, he would swear that *This Is Your Life* was kitsch.
Now everything has turned titanic since his death.
As I soak, foam-ruffled, in the tepid water,
Even the *BE SURE* deodorant bottle
Lies like a toppled king upon the shelf.

# I. The First Hello

Openings and closings. Beginnings and
Endings. Windows. I first shook his cold hand
At our cottage window, one big wind night
When his ghostly face loomed at the pane, right
When it seemed our rural dream might perish.
I pushed the half window out and in he swam,
Surfacing from the darkness like a moon-
Eyed fish. *Tell me, what brought you to a place
Like this?* I leaned full forward, face to face,
And surprised myself by saying *Jesus*.
Pulling back, he studied me from tip to toe
And sighed: *Son, I'll be glad, if that's the case.*
That window, which saw the first hello, was
The window where I'd have to watch him go.

## II. The Grieving Ground

Reaching the why and wherefore of the racket—
A blackbird lying by the garden gate
And her mate protesting from branch to branch—
I sensed something, turned and glanced
And caught him staring from his kitchen window.
I didn't mouth a word or make a sign,
But I knew he knew what was wrong.
He struggled round, put on a scary show,
But failed to stop the sorrow song
Or force the living from the grieving ground.
I shyly watched him shoo at grief,
Remembering the loss of his own wife,
And realised Death, the homeless thief,
Had broken in, squatted and wouldn't leave.

## III. The Starlings

Breakfast dishes washed and dried, he laid his
Cobbled cassie each morning for the birds
With ground-down biscuit bits and breadcrumbs smeared
With butter, rhubarb jam and lemon curd.
In his wing-backed window seat he'd sit and sup
Until the starlings out-muscled the sparrows—
*Hooligans! Greedy guts! You useless shower!*
He was like a poltergeist at work,
With windows banging and blinds rattling,
As he did his best to shift those starlings.
But being cute, they just ebbed in and out
Like oil-slick waves upon the shore, which left him as—
For all his bluster, shouts and growls—
An ornithological King Canute.

## IV. The Lesson

An old-fashioned stickler for hard work and routine—
Everything, inside and outside, sang pristine.
He swept the summer loanen
Until it shone like polished linoleum.
*Breakfast, set the fire, radio, garden ...*
Days were measured to the last degree ...
*Lunchtime, dinnertime, paper-shop, eye-*
*Drops, TV, supper, then bed by ten.*
All things ship-shape was the shipyard rule.
So, the time his son beaked off school
He swore that boy wouldn't act the bastard
And walked him straight back to schoolboy prison.
I wondered if it worked, if he learned his lesson.
*Well, what if I told you he's now a headmaster?*

# V. The Groundsman

His right foot firmly planted on the square,
He crossed lines to tend the green rectangular
Of Cliftonville's Solitude stadium.
Such volunteering was a Lundy sin.
But he'd no time for the balaclava crowd,
Anonymous assassins whose faceless
Death-squads had no provable place
In a province plagued by the shroud—
Both sides were as good or as bad as the other.
Protestant Lone Ranger, it was no bother
When some cowboys blew him head-over-heel,
Out of the tunnel, onto the field,
Like a bloody, big ball of tumbleweed.
It wouldn't take long for his wounds to heal.

## VI. The Cartoon Capers

The bus dropped the kids off, top of the loanen,
At the end of their little school day. They'd zoom
Round the outhouse, fly through the front door,
And dump bags on the hallway floor.
I'd greet them and hug them and smile
As they ventured to visit his wonderland—
A world full of biccies and juices, and
Goodies and baddies, with wizards and witches, *oh my!*
Sat on his settee, cushioned and comfy,
They'd gaze goggle-eyed at TV.
He'd serve them, then sneak out and play
On our window to posse me round for a peek.
We'd clown and we'd caper and mimic
Their features—till they'd rise up and chase us away.

## VII. The Eyewitness

Just six years of age, he was eyewitness
To the first voyage of the world's greatest
Ship. It was so huge it made his heart laugh
To watch it fill the window of the Lough:
From city to sea, from sea to sky,
Full of man's invulnerable majesty.
Now we all know, as it transpired, that they
Were full of infallible fantasy.
*Among them be it*, I can hear him say—
So much for man's invulnerability.
But then I picture him as a boy,
Lying window-eyed on the watching cliff,
Unable to fathom, there in mid-wave,
That ship going down like a faulty toy.

## VIII. The Yardman

Stowed away safely in a box upstairs
(For fear we'd feel he'd put on airs),
The man who didn't even own a car,
Owned a letter signed, 'Elizabeth R.'
She'd sealed his British Empire Medal
For services to shipping at Harland & Wolff.
Though proud, he required no Royal proof
Of his place in the Belfast shipyard's tidal
Crews. Nicknamed 'The Whippet' for laddering
Speed—boiler-room, top deck, to the quay—
The gifted souvenir considered savvy
Was David Hammond's 'The Boat Factory'.
*His* 'John Hancock' proved fit for friends to see:
'For Billy, who knows it all. Best, Davy.'

## IX. The Back Garden

Sweat falling from his brow onto cold clay,
He turned the earth at the end of the day.
Townie, with appetite for country work,
He used the spade and graipe like knife and fork.
Upending moist heads of Medusa loam,
He finger-sieved fat garden worms and weeds
That had made a mess of his perfect beds,
Stripping them like snakes from a gorgon's comb.
My kids were dumbstruck—both mouths wide open—
As he hung worms from the cherry blossom.
When evening fell, I would call out their names—
He'd point their hiding place without one word,
Then plant his spade like a battlefield sword,
And watch the dying sun go down in flames.

## X. The Last Look

Feeling his heart's battery running down,
He took me with him for a dander round
The fields to see his childhood home again.
We stood in sad ruins in soft Irish rain
With two dappled stallions who watched us scan
Newspapers that lined the walls and conjured
Up bloody ghosts of the dead and injured
From two World Wars. The horses had moved in.
We pottered homeward by the sandy street
Where waves dropped pearly bracelets at his feet,
And on the Gobbins headland ridge-trees shot
Back weathered wind-swept branches in salute.
We turned away—but not before his hot
Eyes had set longingly on one last look.

# XI. The Loved Ephemeral

I cried my eyes out at the funeral—
Earthbound tears for the loved ephemeral—
Sitting near the rear of the congregation,
Unable to match their restraint of emotion:
That Ulster Presbyterian virtue,
Fostered from cradle to grave,
By people who'd flourish backhanded waves
At the playing of heartstrings in public view.
Some sneaked looks at me over their shoulder,
The old were subtle, the younger bolder.
Imagine what they would have thought
If those tsunami tears had built and built,
Lifting his coffin from its catafalque
And carrying it homeward up Belfast Lough.

# XII. The Dream of Goodbye

In the dream world, he said goodbye for good.
It played itself out like a rehearsal would—
The knock at the door, the hurry round,
The dreadful heartsick fear of what we'd find.
We found him dead upon his flooring,
Beside his bed, the faintest photocopy
Of himself, an image from Fellini,
Not lying really, more like hovering.
When the neighbour went downstairs to phone,
She left us, momentarily, on our own,
Dreamtime still. Then my heart began to hum
As he opened his eyes, opened his mouth,
And from our loosened tongues the truth
Eased out: *I love you, Billy*; and, *I love you, son.*

# XIII. The Changeful Tap

The water would suddenly thin to a trickle,
Some summer evenings while filling the kettle—
It took an eternity just to make tea.
And I'd know with an absolute certainty
He'd made his way back to the garden
To toddle around the immaculate rows,
To sprinkle the heads of infant flowers
From the font of his watering can.
It was such chores that kept him happy.
Still, I'd secretly curse our shared supply
And covet the moment when I'd have control.
But nowadays reaching to turn on the tap,
I sometimes fall for the futile hope
The running water might suddenly slow.

## XIV. The Ghosts Remain

How sadly once familiar things seem strange—
How much changes for the worse, in our eyes,
Of the homes we love and leave. It's as if
This is the only way to cope with why we left:
Returning to find them neglected or
Re-arranged; not surviving all that well
Without us. It means that we can tell
Ourselves how blessed we definitely are
To have left them trailing in our wake,
Sailing off for Elsewhere, waltzing with Fate.
But then, ghosts of ourselves and of old friends
Surface round us, smiling gently—they know
That our indifference is mostly show:
And know they will be with us when it ends.

# Epilogue: The Double Crown

Sometimes I feel like I let you down in
The end, old friend, spending time out running
Around with other best friends. I guess I
Never learned from the late neglect of my
Lonely grandmother. Funny, last word I
Shared with her over the phone was *Jesus*.
Just in case I'm right—if I let us
Down in life—I hope you'll accept poetry
In the hereafter as poor recompense
From the man you mentored who's seen some sense.
So take this double crown (wreathed at each end)
And you wear yours, and I'll wear mine
And let's break bread together across space and time:
Me, in the here-now; you, in the there-then.

# The Recovery

*for JB & AM*

The bed had become his whole home.
Then one morning, late, he pulled back

The covers, like he was opening a garden gate,
Strode across the lawn-lush carpet to the veranda

Of his desk, sat down, took up his pen,
And sent it sailing on the ocean page.

# Whale

Waiting for my students to gather,
I was silently lamenting how
Blue whales can't hear each other

Sing, as they once were able
To do, freely, from ocean to ocean
Across our watery globe

'Cause we've drowned the seven seas
In an incessant babble,
When a student cruised into class

With a cell shell glued to her ear.
When I casually asked if she'd tell us
Who she was speaking to, her

Eyebrows lifted and her face flushed
As she pointed to another girl
Sitting with her back to the wall, and gushed,

*Her!* We all smiled. But I knew well,
That class was going to hear the tale
'Failing Songs of the Great Blue Whale'.

# Among the Lavender

Honeybees spend their busy day
Hovering among the lavender
With constant co-workers for company.

Each a natural-born spacewalker,
They lend the light leaves some sway
As they drift from flower to flower.

For them, perhaps, the pale purple
Of the holy herb is just
Another colour, and the beautiful

Fragrance may be only a wind-blown
Aroma-sugar aimed solely at us,
But from sunup to sundown

Honeybees love lavender and toil together
For the good of the whole hive.
Come daligone, a few workaholics are

Left drone-dozy on a psychedelic buzz,
Dream-heavy with sweet nectarmares
On their soft perfumy beds.

What the hive finally harvests,
The lavender won't miss.
Lavender exists for this.

# Thieves Like Us

Well into evening, we crossed into Estrie, Quebec's bucolic land of Victorian mansions, where Mary's a fountain and Jesus a garden gnome. We'd driven north from Thoreau's Concord, up through wooded Vermont and Maine, following the trail of rich Confederates who—lowering their blinds as they passed through New England—trundled the rails in private coaches for summering free of white hot weather and 'dastardly Yankees'.

We left the main road at sleepy Barnston, veered over to the verge of a farmer's field and silenced the car. Peering past the black-and-white mapped sides of curious cattle, we were struck by an unusual outhouse, a round barn, a thing we had heard of but never seen. Built with wafer-thin window slits and nipple-topped, as if bell-belfried, it was an unearthly marriage of mosque and Martello tower. Its roundness arose from the local belief that the Devil hides in corners—one more strange version of voodoo, since the book has him prince of this globular world and the sightless seer of paradise has written that Heaven is square. After she took the holiday snap, we chit-chatted, until I murmured that our hearts mustn't be round. After that, nothing more seemed sayable.

Slowly we became aware of a low ringing, the gentle tambourine jingle of the cicada, and then, lifting our eyes, we feasted on the eucharist of the full moon that blazed over everything, doing its best to salve the soul. Refreshed, I fired the ignition, and, as she held my free hand in hers, we pressed on, steering for Kingston, halfway on our journey home.

# The Dead Bride

*for Geoffrey Hill*


In far-off Carolina,
On the roadside turret
Of our evening porch,

I found this poem
When I instinctively
Lifted your open book

And clapped it shut
To trap
A dithery mosquito.

When I re-opened the paper tomb,
There he was,
The dark suitor,

Pinned back
Against the thin sheet,
Full blood bags

Unbelievably spilled
Across
The predestined verse:

'So white I was, he would have me cry
*Unclean!* Murderously
To heal me with far-fetched blood'.

# Texts

*for Alan Mearns*


Just sieving the daily dust, panning for poems ...
*Sent*

Last night, the whole forest
moved and shook itself
like a huge drenched dog.
*Sent*

... all night, skin-tight, hold-warm,
sheet-surf rippling and rolling
towards the coasts of love ...
*Sent*

Rising and falling on the chest-swells,
our wee one sleeps on love-liners, human oceans.
*Sent*

Too tired to deal with the fuss,
we've let the bairn bed down
in the valley of himself
between the two mountains of us.
*Sent*

I love those late night
living room light bulbs,
those insomnia suns.
*Sent*

It doesn't matter how vast it is 'out there'.
We all know the 'in here' is vaster.
*Sent*

It's dark, but what's 'missing' in the Universe
truly matters ... works just as well
for what's left out of one good verse.
*Sent*

Tornadoes: wind-ropes,
shower-room towels, for real.
*Sent*

Night sheets are dune-ribbed sands,
high Himalayan ranges.
*Sent*

There's no place left for me at the Mall
since Waldenbooks just up and left.
*Sent*

Hard to swallow the gun-lover's dictum—
'The gun is always an innocent victim'.
*Sent*

Does everything earthly also yearn to go off with a bang?
*Sent*

From the darkling porch on rainy nights,
I watch cars photocopying the glassy streets.
*Sent*

Somewhere between Pound and Williams,
nearly every thing is 'like a',
... things are seldom what they are.
*Sent*

I said, *Poetry? Poetry?*
*Poetry is verbal mathematics,*
*the algebra of the soul!* Then fled.
*Sent*

What we deeply believe is right today
is often deeply wrong tomorrow—
the shifting sands of scientific inquiry ...
*Sent*

An instant after they strike ground,
each raindrop wears a rainy crown.
*Sent*

The streets may well be paved with it,
but gold is not the currency of Heaven.
*Sent*

Good poets are ventriloquists
and ev'ry dummy fits their fists.
*Sent*

One can only pour so much love into a word ...
but everything that's left out survives, unheard.
*Sent*

Poetry's tough.  It won't let you bully folk
into liking it.  It's all about love.
*Sent*

Everything's a preparation for separation.
*Sent*

Fidelity to poetry
is such a healthy
madness ...

# The Clock Flower

As far as the rest of the universe is concerned,
Maybe we're like the feather-fluff of the clock flower,

The ghostly snow-sphere of the dying dandelion
That the child holds up in wide-eyed wonder,

Which the mother says to blow on to tell the time
By how many breath-blows it takes before the airy seed

All flies away, leaving her child clutching a bare stem.

And where our humanness might go, who knows?
And when it lands—takes root—what grows?

# Cardboard

Last night, while leisurely reading on the toilet,
I became aware of a strange heat against my bare right
Leg, caused by the cardboard side of a huge Huggies

Diaper box, emblazoned with the promise, Snug and Dry.
I immediately thought of people living in cardboard cities;
Of just how grateful one could be for cardboard warmth.

I was re-reading Wordsworth's 'Tintern Abbey',
About the *still, sad music of humanity,*
About its *ample power / to chasten and subdue.*

When I finished, and washed my hands, and brushed my teeth,
A small quiet voice seemed to almost audibly say—
Face it; life's only ever really good, if it's good for you.

# Ever Émigrés

Always breathtaking when kings of the passerines
Begin to gather on local telegraph wires,
Slick squadrons somersaulting into lines

For their autumnal assault on the south.
Easy to cast them as crotchets and quavers,
But the two-fisted wind-grip of Ulster's north-

East makes them swivel like foosball figures
As they rev up for take-off for Africa.
Like us Irish, swallows and books are ever émigrés,

And I imagine my own book-flock lining up in Belfast
Mist for their trans-Atlantic flight to America.
Not all make it, though thousands do, returning to roost

In western nests, under familiar wooden eaves.
As I spread their paper wings, strum folio feathers,
The heart sings and soars over the mind's dark seas.

# St Francis and the Kisses

Leaves from the Japanese maple have perished,
Some dry-scrunched, some burgundy-powdered,
Deep pink-pastel resin dusting the dainty feet
Of our garden genie, hooded, head-bent, Crossed.
Cold contemplative, bird-lover, folds of his stone robes
Garden-algaed, in gentle green-greyed waves
Rolling round him, he's reminiscent of a Zeppelin
Cover or an elfin enchanter from a famous fiction.

My youngest always makes his way over to him,
Bends down and looks him in the eye, smiling,
Puts an arm around his shoulders, kisses him on his crown.
Though I knew that this would likely end up in a poem,
It was waiting for its mirror in my older son,
Bending over me in front of the stereo station,
Blessing me—in my head-down, cupped-chin slumber
Before slipping to his holiday bed—with a kiss I remember.

# Planted

*We have no prairies*
*To slice a big sun at evening*
      —Seamus Heaney, 'Bogland'

I

We have no porches to share a slice of melon on back home,
To sit on to watch the sun go down, least not where I come from:
No tree frogs, no cicadas, no rhythmic rattling in treetops.
Closest we come to them are the squeaky brakes of passing cars,
Or the sing-song goings-on of late evening's emptying bars.
And no fireflies. Lightning bugs. Blinking on and off like sudden
Thoughts. Nearest we come to them is on soggy, foggy nights when
Unmanned, landlocked lighthouses attempt to keep us off the rocks.

II

Planted here, though, enjoying the electrons of evening,
I can picture certain characters from home as they lean
Against door lintels, or perch on front-step chairs and look out,
Or gather on public benches on the outskirts of town
To swap stories, then silently stare at thinning traffic,
Well past sundown, under the scrubbed spud of a summer moon.
I probably share some genes with such curbside Calvinists,
Happy to sit and watch as heat waves shiver into mist.

# One to Another

*for Lori & Clay Templeton*

Found sitting a Carolina spell, thinking how
We're either building up or bringing down,
When my neighbour from across the way

Raises his hand and shares a wordless wave.
I raise mine silently and bounce it back,
Happy to feel the force of his friendly move,

That costs us nothing when we give it up:
The kind of exchange I used to have
With Ulster country people as they sat

Upon their trundling tractors on rural roads
Or closed their gates on cattle fields,
Repaying urban patience with a hand and nod.

It's good to put our hands up in this way,
To see ourselves simply mirrored in another,
As naturally as one wave will make its way

From one unforgotten seashore to another.

# Redbreast

Memorial Day. Mown grass. Wee man down for doze.
I'm sitting on the evening porch; it's humid, but nice.
A rising breeze riffles my magazines like flags.

Only garden drama centres on the newborn robin
Who couldn't be more obviously trusting, more exposed,
Caught out in the open, perched on the low garden

Wall. Clearly not a flier, yet. I'm busily distracting
The feline who shares our porch, in hope that the fledgling
Can quickly find its wings. The parents are crisscrossing

Anxiously overhead, sounding their alarms, shouting
Support from the safety of trees. Wonderful to think
That the last thing little redbreast has to fear at this time,

Surrounded by all natural perils—the unfriendly blood
Of the air; toying cat claws on the ground—is human.
I raise my brimming glass in thankfulness and drain it good.

# Leaves

Under the thinning canopy of autumn trees,
I watch over my son while he plays in the leaves.

His blossoming boyhood is a blessing to see,
In the light of those leaves which are falling from me.

# Beseech

*for Seth Collings Hawkins*

Dangerous to entrust the grains of truth
To the hourglass hands of us humans.
I am verily heartsick of party politics,
Of constitutional charades, and so-called
Social posts from our puritanical patriots
Or baby-boomers flirting with pat-riots—

The positively right telling the other
That they're so black-and-white-ly wrong.
I have seen it, and I've heard it all before,
And sadly not in another lifetime.
I sympathise with those who know that money
Talks, and that it stinks, and that the love of it

Is a hothouse for the flowers of evil.
I'm with those who know that simply holding on
Is all that they've got, or are ever likely to get,
And that faithful letting go is their only holding on.
And I remember the great dissenter, John Hewitt,
Cleverly quoting Cromwell—demonic to Catholics—

In an interview with Dublin's *Irish Times,*
Referencing his exhortation to the Presbyterians
Of Scotland: *I beseech you in the bowels of Christ*
*Think it possible you may be mistaken.*
If even Cromwell could conceive of the second guess,
Isn't it about time that we all did the same?

# For All Is There

*Surf City, NC, Summer 2013*

As the old full moon succumbs to cloud,
leaving a nicotine stain in its shroud,
I lift my glassy eyes to the sound shore,
where every light's a Ferris-wheel or clock flower.

Up this high, ear-level with tree frogs and cicadas,
I have never heard them so interrupt thought.
Hickory-porched, they're only a background comfort,
no louder than those childhood pull-back drags

we would rev and race across the scullery floor.
Old Horace said that no poems worth their
salt were ever written by drinkers of water.
Sounds like a Bukowski bite, a faithful follower

of the blushful glass ... and just as soon
as now, clamourous clouds close the sky dome,
and bolt lightning turns the lightless wetland
into a floodlit field, sending any stranded

sinners onto their hopeful hands and knees.
But from this balcony tonight, I could happily
drama-fall into the hands and arms of the electric air
and fully trust the unseen. For all is there.

# Lent

Few things as eye-soothing as dying light
From fall's show, temporally on loan.
The trees that line the avenue tonight
Have lost the many colours they have worn
With such dapper-dazzle during the day.
The sun, wardrobe manager of daytime,
Is the robber who has left them poorly
Dressed in the post-show monochrome evening.
The waning moon, lunula of lent light,
One half lit, the other blackened by night,
Portrays this substance and shadow of life,
And simply *is*, in sunshine and in shade.
While we swing wildly from singing to strife,
Forgetful that we're similarly made.

# A Dark Leaf

*for Ross Wilson*

Along the alley of our avenue,
Birds flicker nervously between tall trees,
Nests bobbing under the black-and-blue
Of a stormful sky. The high branch-kelp sways
In the lifting wind-wave, delivering
A dark leaf through the mailbox of my porch,
Dropping onto my notebook, like a sign.
Everything is darkening. Lightning flirts
With telegraph poles. Thunder-balls rumble
The bowling lanes overhead, their mumble
Silencing the cooing of a dove.
Here comes the rain, so redolent of home.
Odd, the things we miss of the things we love.
Time to pack up and go inside, alone.

# So I Wish

Matthew, my oldest
son's a proper poet
now, something that
seems incredible
somehow, though I
should have known
that when he published
a poem of mine
upon his ribs
that poetry had
announced itself
in residence
beneath the skin.

Then I come
into the room,
just now, to find
Micah, my youngest,
squatting on the floor
beside his drawing pad.
He has become bored
with the paper page
and has turned
the inky pen upon himself:
arms, legs, feet, toes—
the freehand abandon
of toddler tattoos.

And then I recall
that the Father's laws
are written not upon
the page nor on the skin
but deeper down,
within, in ink
the colour of
our deepest sin, in
heart-red that rolls round
the veins, seals the soul,
and so I wish my sons both
poetry, art, and the Word
that makes them whole.

# Just Enough

*for Angela Beaver Simmons*

Who knows what my neighbour's kitchen holds
Of love or loss, of longing or loneliness,

Or of any clichéd combination of the above.
But as the darkness draws itself down,

Light burns across the kitchen borders
Onto the window-high azaleas

In sufficient excess to flame the flowery
Promise just enough to catch my weary eye,

To resurrect my buried thankfulness,
To rekindle my own love affair with desire.

# Neighbourhood

I dwell in a neighbourhood where most driveways
are laid with white marble stones of a kind which
are normally raked over posh people's graves

and where the house opposite is a dead ringer for
the only home I could ever draw easily at school—
roofed square, four windows, winding pathway to door—

and where the green grassy garden is treated to a trim
never having been left long enough to merit a cut
and where I can sit on my porch and read and dream

and sip chilled wine for hours on end while tree frogs
and cicadas blend their comforting evening fugue
and the only thing to fear is the mighty mosquito ...

what a change from the streets of my Rathcoole childhood
when if I stood at our door and simply gazed out
I'd be greeted with, *Who the fuck are you lookin' at?*

# Tour of Fire

Eleventh Night peaks. The Twelfth has come. Torches
Are lit and thrust into the driest branches
Of the pagan pyre. Time for the tour of fire.
Inferno in every window; wood and tyres
Sending smoke signals up into the night sky.
Proud Papal effigies preparing to die.
Bewildered Mormons, Jehovah Witnesses,
Looking down from their balcony maisonettes.
Loyal players in these fiery mirror-halls,
The usual suspects are fanning the flames:
The accordionist, the preacher, the drunk,
The skinhead, the hood, and the grammar school punk;
The flirt, the millie, and the token taig
(Suffered, good-humouredly, when things aren't too bad);
The dole-soul, the work-shy, and the work-is-done,
The mason, the slapper, and off-duty policeman;
All swaying and singing to Loyalist songs
Blaring from bass-booming home radiograms—
Some placed on the paths like musical coffins,
Tight owners sat on them, holding their half'ins.
        There are the beer-bellied boys, low-chested athletes,
Tenants tins stamped with girls in scant panties,
And their wives swigging their wee Smirnoff's and Cokes,
Relaxing for the moment, sharing some jokes,
But secretly tuned to their man's rising laugh,
Some fearing the cost of this night's aftermath.
To drown such fears, there's Pernod and blackcurrant,
Leg-openers to maybe spare the children ...
But all that's in the future, the night's still young,
Time for girlie banter about the 'well-hung' ...
        Coffin-nail of choice is Embassy Regal—
Or Embassy Red if the wallet's able—
No. 6 or Players or Rothman's King Size
For highfalutin types with gold in their eyes,
Voluptuous women with bare bosom soufflés
Who know that their jiggle is mankind's heart-prize.
People suck on cancer sticks, long, hard and strong,
To raise themselves out of a houseful of wrong.

But let's give a nick to the Gallagher's weed
And return to the main act played on the green.
        To 'King' Billy and Bobby, and big Davy
Who'd savour the chance to mangle a Mickey.
They're seated around the 'top table', flanking
The main paramilitary man, who's yanking
Their chains with sinister banter to keep them
In check, making sure they're reminded it's him
That they owe loyalty to—lest they forget.
Not easy to do, considering the state
Of their mucker's face who had made the mistake
Of hitting the wrong guy a dig in the bake.
And there are plenty of youthful replacements,
Now sniffing round wee girls like dogs with two dicks:
Schoolgirls stretching their long chewing gum high wires
From hands to mouths, with confident, cheeky smiles,
Teen titties on show … but they don't realise
That their precious hymens are playing with fire.
Though some have clearly gone off to the races,
Those marks might be passion-poppies … or bruises …
*Ack, you can't talk to them at this age!* I hear
Big Sadie say, sidling up to bend my ear,
Reminding me to remember my teenage
Years, when such schoolgirls starred in my own wet dreams.
Then she smiles and suggests that we let them run on,
And pray that it amounts to no more than fun.
*It's better than being alone like Ms. Ward—*
*Soaks her dildos in vinegar to keep them hard!*
        But to get the whole truth, come a bit closer,
And witness the things surrounding love's bonfire.
See the innocent caught in the web of life,
Not one thing or other, not suited for strife,
Yet playing their part in the Protestant scene,
Being born in Rathcoole, and not Skibbereen.
Doubtless they're characters that carry some hope,
Who can look at their mates and dare to say, nope
That's not what I'm into, I mean no offense,
But hating a Catholic just makes no sense.

(But then that's easy when Republican guns
Are not pointed at your own flesh-and-blood ones.)
It's not all about Billy-boys, birds and booze.
There are ordinary heroes here because
It's their community, for good or for ill,
And they won't surrender their traditional
Celebrations totally to the dark side—
Would be easier to sit at home and hide.
See doting grandkids on grandparent's knees.
Hear the old ones swapping childhood memories.
Watch playground sweethearts holding hands in public,
Willingly running the wolf-whistle gauntlet.
See the 'deeps' in their duffle-coats sneaking
A joint, who can't for the life of them quite see
The point, but they've left their hippy incense-dark,
Unable to resist the communal lark,
For despite education's enlightenment,
They're still drawn to the Eleventh excitement.
        Whiff the irresistible aromas from
The welcome wagon-train of lay-by chip-vans,
Serving gravy chips, curry chips, fish suppers,
Pasties, sausages, bacon sodas, burgers,
Fanta, Coke, Iron Brew, Lilt, and Seven-Up,
Ulster cheddar and cold cuts in big Belfast baps.
See kids queuing for cones from Mr. Whippy,
'99' pokes with flakes and chocolatey
Sprinkles, or flake-less but with tarn in top
Of strawberry or of raspberry syrup,
Or feasting on lollies like Seajet, Quencher,
Cornetto, Fab, Rocket, Magnum and Joker,
Choc Ice, Ice Pop, the ice-cream harmonica—
Wafered slabs of mouth-watering vanilla.
And Candy Floss! E number-less nebulas!
Pink pillars of creation where sugar's
Born! Formed by hands circling in widening gyres,
Kids crave second helpings of this edible air.
        (Love the banter between old primary school mates,
Now separated by 11-Plus Tests,

Swappin' slaggin's alongside the ice-cream van:
*It's Strider the Slider & Vanilla the Man!*
Without missing a beat, the ball's back with grins:
*It's The Wallypops & The Skinhead Supremes!*)
      The mobile shop that's a permanent fixture,
Is also getting well in on the picture,
Supplying the adults with mixers and cigs,
Mining the pocket money gold rush of kids
Who've struck it rich from half-blocked uncles and aunts.
With such dosh now burning a hole in their pants,
The shop is thankfully well-stocked and ready—
A cornucopia of confectionary!
There are Lucky Bags, Wine Gums, Chelsea Whoppers,
Sports Mixture, Black Jacks, Fruit Salad and Gob Stoppers,
Sherbet Fountains, Dib Dabs, Lucky Mines, Cola
Bottles, Flumps, Fruit Gums, Munchies and Mintola,
Fruit Pastilles, Fruitella and 10p mixes,
Bounty Bar, Golden Cup, Crunchie and Twix,
Galaxy, Picnic, Opal Fruits and Mars Bars,
Aero, Love Hearts, Caramel, Chocolate Éclairs,
Curly Wurly, Fry's Cream, Flake and Marathon,
Milky Bar, Milky Way, and the Toblerone!
As many sweeties as wild flowers of the Burren—
Don't have all night to stand here and name them …
(Keep those health-wise *tut, tuts* in suburbia—
Sometimes these kids' only comfort is sugar.)
      My granny and granda have just dandered up—
It's strictly Tetley tea in their drinking cups.
Salt-of-the-earth Ulster-Scots, country people,
Who carry the weather of their own locale
Like a breath of fresh air into this scene
And lend it some semblance of real dignity.
Granda's the quiet one, but granny's a talker
And though a churchgoer, nothing can shock her,
No, not even big Sadie and her harem
Of housewives come over to see how she's been.
      The fire's really raging by now, it's burning
Its way through the telegraph wires, and singeing

The eyebrows on reddening faces of folk
Too tipsy to care; and of proud kids who've built
The bonie and are innocently basking
In the glow of watching their parents' good time.
It's blistering paintwork on bonie-side homes
And fracturing windows in their living rooms.
But, like Christmas, Eleventh Night comes round just
Once a year: as then, so now, in God they trust
To foot the bill for any bonie damage,
Which won't be much as long as there's no rampage
Of eejit teenagers who can't hold their drink.
And to speak of some damage, I hate to think
Of blood spilled on the green before the night's out
But it happens, and's nearly always about
Someone caught putting their hands where they shouldn't.
It's always a clash with randy Protestant
Celebrity brethren blown in from Scotland
To add some Bannockburn to the Twelfth Day bands.
Their kilts and their sporrans can turn women's heads
And make them unmindful of their marriage beds.
It never ends well, but's mostly forgotten—
There's serious marching to do come morning.
          Let's leave the tour here at the height of the night;
Hope that the just will be allowed to sleep tight.
While, for some, it's all downhill from here to dawn,
For the young fire-builders, it's ladders to heaven—
It's hard to fathom, but part of the picture:
Kids are Cowboys and Indians, not just your
Prods versus Taigs of the grown-up condition.
The night truly begins for bonfire children
When the adults head off to parties or bed—
Time for baking big spuds in the dying red
Embers, and then feeding the flames to make
Sure that their bonfire survives until daybreak.
They've given their all for the Loyalist cause
Not with any prejudicial malice, as
Many of their parents and siblings have done,
But because they have been given permission

To be hunters and gatherers, selected,
Yes, by tribal grown-ups to help them erect
Monuments of Protestant magnificence,
But outside of flirting with fire, there's no sense
Of real premeditated, knowledgeable
Hatred directed through flames to those unable
To get housed by the Housing Executive—
At this stage, they're happy to live and let live.

# NHOJ

I'm big McClatchy and I don't give a fuck,
Except for your bird if she's fit for a buck.
I tattooed my own name on my forehead once
—Just actin' the lig, like, playin' the dunce—
It was a wee homemade job, done at the house,
And I managed to screw up my own name—twice.
When I finally nailed it, it looked fuckin' well,
Except for the fact it was so hard to tell
('Cause it looked more like some stupid fenian scrawl)
If it was written in proper English at all.
So I asked my mates for their opinion
And was pissed off to see them all fall about laughin'.
But they did let me know that I'd got it wrong—
Instead of 'JOHN', it really read 'NHOJ'.
You can imagine my fuckin' horror …
Though it taught me NEVER to trust in the mirror.

# Bones and Blood

My bones are pavement, and my blood cement,
I'm the Protestant half of an Irish lament.
From the Rathcoole housing estate, I'm torn,
By way of Dromara and the Mountains of Mourne.
        Within one-nine-six, on Derrycoole Way,
I made my memories, and remember the day
That a workman left footprints forevermore
Upon the unset pathway to our front door;
Footprints I knew would be someone's undoing
If they were not watching where they were going:
Sunk down in cement by some Immanent Will
For my brother, Annesley, who was nearly killed
When he went for a trip, and had a great fall,
Headfirst through the glass door and into our hall,
Because he was basically being a get
To beat me to money to buy a Seajet.
Being hard on his heels, I witnessed it all—
Saw him bloodied, lifeless, and flat on the floor,
Face-shrouded in the lace curtain that adorned
Our front door. But you could never keep him down
And out; he was soon up and washed and away—
Good prep for a boy who would face the IRA.
        Much stranger than fiction, the funniest thing
Was that our family had been preparing
For days for something similar to happen
To me, set down in stone by a prediction
Made by my Presbyterian grandmother,
Who would work herself up into a lather
Because of her unfortunate psychic powers
That would often keep her awake for long hours
Worrying about the poor apparitions
From her vivid, dream-given revelations.
        Although she couldn't say when or where or why,
My granny foresaw airplanes fall from the sky,
And prophesied the time when a spoil-tip slipped down
To stop up young mouths in a coal mining town.
She said she had dreamt that an ominous cloud
Grew bigger and darker and covered a crowd
Of innocent children sat in a room

And brought them black rain from the kingdom of doom ...
She swore they were singing a beautiful hymn
With voices like birds warbling sweetly in whin.
The Aberfan disaster would strike home each year
When Welsh male voice choirs would bring down a tear.
          But as sure as such dreams, every prediction
Would be fulfilled with a different victim
Suffering the bad (never good) of any
Dream scenario phoned through by my granny
To a daughter, son or other relation—
I had been earmarked for Annesley's misfortune.

# The Deep Field

Blurry Christmas tree lights in the corner gloom
Become the Hubble deep field, making this room
A portal through which I travel back in time
To seek out the company of my own kind.
      Early Christmas Eve; my young brother and I
Are already in bed, the only night my
Parents knew we'd volunteer to climb the stairs
Without the need for either of their orders.
I'm the oldest by three whole years, coming ten,
Old enough to know the saddest truth by then:
That Santa Claus is just a storybook sham,
Another figment of human invention.
But I was predestined to be a friend of
The imagination; found myself in love
With things invisible to sense and to plain
Sight—had reinvented him; believed again.
      I haven't yet moved into the box room. I'm
Still sharing a bedroom, glad that at bedtime
I can safely ask that the landing light be
Left on and blame it on my brother, as he
Still has an excuse for not liking the dark.
Asking is no problem when dad is at work.
But tonight, I know that my dad's Santa Claus,
And my about-to-burst heart's primed with applause.
      Lying beside my brother in semi-gloom,
I can hear sounds rising from the living room:
Comforting parental happy talk and low
Canned laughter from a comedy Christmas show
Everyone liked—the great Morecambe and Wise ...
Though my brother gets beaten by sleep, my eyes
Are set firmly on the prize of Christmas morn.
I know we can't get up until after dawn,
But the very second that daylight comes round,
We both race downstairs without touching the ground.
      Though working class kids, not mammon anointed,
I can honestly say we aren't disappointed:
We get toy soldiers, and football boots, and kits,
Cool games, and annuals, and even two bikes.
Our mum and dad rise to look at our faces,

Then head back to bed to resume their places
In a dream world that we wouldn't begrudge them,
Since they've left us in our version of heaven.
        Before the long day's out, before bed seems good,
We turn our attention to kids' Christmas food:
Not turkey and stuffing with gravy and peas,
But from padding presents left under the tree—
Selection boxes created perfectly,
Full of Mars Bars, Milky Ways and Galaxys.

# The Alpha

It always has the promise of beginning,
Going down to the Alpha of an evening,
Rushing into the plush-pile, hoovered splendour
Of that well-carpeted cinema foyer,
An entrance large-postered with Hollywood greats
And lined with glassed counters for tickets and treats.
     Pop-corned and fizzy-drinked, we welcome the dark.
A torchy shines us to our seats. We shuffle-walk
Past half-risen fellow torn ticket holders
Who just conceal the narkiness that smoulders
Beneath their tight-lipped smiles. We can't care less.
We're focused on our mission to see the best
That Hollywood has prepared for us tonight.
Subtly choosing seats, with 'best' mates left and right,
We elbow in to thole the advertisements,
Which merely serve to stoke our core excitement.
Anytime now, the magic curtains will close,
And though we are sitting, we'll be on our toes
For the lights to dim and the curtains to open.
And here it comes! The regal, roaring lion!
Calling us into the land of make-believe,
Which is somehow always better than where we live.
     Tonight, we're in the balcony, not the stalls,
So we get to pause and muster up the balls
To send our sticky lollies sky-rocketing
In the dark, raining down on the plebs below.
We snigger at the shouts and simply lie low,
Poker-faced in the torchlight that scans our row.
Then it's back to business and on with the show.
     This night, per usual, we're put through the mill,
Torn between laughter and tears, good and the ill,
But left believing that good guys always win.
There *will* be last minute punishment for sin.
The movie finishes, the titles descend,
And it draws to a close with two words: THE END.
     But then that's just the start of the beginning,
For when we are young we are always winning.
The curtains close, and the Anthem begins, but

We're nowhere to be seen, being up and out
To round up the dregs of our pocket money
To bag us some chips from the Alpha café.
Then we run like the wind straight out the front doors
With our top-buttoned, hooded duffle-coat cloaks
Flowing behind us as we act out our scenes—
Full of Cowboys and Indians, Kings and Queens,
Goodies and Baddies—in our innocent minds,
Realer than real ....... But we can't foresee the times
When the Alpha is a drinking den, drunken
Hoods being all the show, while true working
Men stay home to shelter their wives and children:
Not matinee men; but heroes, in the end.

# Bullets or Bats

Big Bobby Cain strolled down to The Diamond to
Seek some advice from one of the chosen few—
A Catholic solicitor that was allowed
To peddle his wares with the Protestant crowd
('Cause even the dogs knew that Taigs knew their rights).
       Ushered in by a cute wee thing in black tights,
And greeted by a smile and a handshake, he
Joked that the lawyer'd forgotten Masonry.
Grinning, the lawyer asked Bobby what he could
Do him for. Bobby then cleared his throat and said
That the lawyer might want to consider it
As being 'off the record', if he knew what
He meant. The lawyer then mimicked turning off
His recorder, and prepared to hear something rough.
       The form was that Bobby had made a mistake
That meant that both of his knees would have to break
Before his wrong could be put right. He had been
Out on the razzle one night at the Ardeen
Hall, and had drunkenly fell in with a doll
Who had never slept with her arse to the wall—
Problem being, she was married to his best
Mate, who was spending his time down in the Kesh
For giving his all for the Loyalist cause.
(It's easy to imagine the pregnant pause.)
His mate didn't give two shites for his hoor at home,
But such behaviour 'the boys' couldn't condone.
The lawyer leant forward and nervously asked
What exactly Bobby thought was his task.
       In a nutshell—in terms of the compensation,
Should he choose bullets or bats? So you can
Picture the look on the solicitor's bake—
A classic case of an oul Del Boy double-take—
As he slumped back bewildered into his chair.
Bobby understood that it was hardly fair—
The proverbial darkie's arse in moonlight—
To ask him the question, but in the light
Of the fact that a big payout was comin',
He thought the lawyer might fancy some action.

The lawyer 'hadn't heard the conversation',
But agreed to take a piece of the action.
          Bats over bullets was apparently best
To maximise coffers from the compo chest.
Though bullets were obviously dangerous,
The bats produced unpredictable messes,
And there'd be brownie points from the assessors
For extra trauma from hands-on aggressors.
So Bobby accepted the lawman's advice
And cast in his lot with bats' roll of the dice.
He phoned 'the boys' to pass on his decision,
And then went to bed with the television.
          Next day he was woken by his old mother
Who sensed that he was in some kind of bother
Because of the awkwardness of the nervous
Crew that had just interrupted her breakfast.
Bobby reassured her not to be worried,
And got into his daily duds and hurried
Downstairs to see who'd been sent to do the job—
He was relieved to see mates filling their gobs.
          There sat Mr. Red, Mr. White and Mr. Blue,
Three of the local smalltime hoods, sent round to
Administer Bobby's punishment beating.
The fact that the same doll had been giving
All three of them the same kind of attention
Was neither here nor there, not worth a mention—
The big lad's mistake was to go and get caught.
Feeling sorry for their oul mucker, they brought
Him some 'anesthesia'—gold whiskey, wine
And beer, and made him to promise, by the time
They'd return later that day, that he'd have them
Beaten down his fat neck to help numb the pain.
His ma was like a second mum to them all,
So he should pack her off to the bingo hall.
          He thanked them, though he worried that the booze would
Make him bleed a bit more, but they swore blind they'd
Get an ambulance the minute they were done—
There'd be no body when his mother got home.

They'd also take care not to leave a real mess,
To spare his mother any needless distress.
With all that being said, they showed themselves out,
And left their oul mucker to his drinking bout.
      To cut a long story short, they shattered his knees—
Three men who couldn't punch through wet paper bags ...
But they kept to their word, for what it was worth—
He got help and survived by the skin of his teeth.
Once able, he hobbled out to cash his 'winnin's',
And was greeted by a gang of wee hallions
Who ran shouting round the shops, in Rathcoole rain:
*Look at big Bobby, and his best mate—Cane!*

# Heart Ache

Uniformed us, sweating in a mobile hut
Waiting for our English teacher to show up,
Dying to begin to torture the old fool:
Lucky 'Troubles' children, country grammar school
Kids who escaped from the massacre on a
Daily basis; bright teenagers who'd passed the
Eleven Plus test or, like *moi*, had fluffed it
But benefitted from parents who'd paid out
Money they couldn't afford to try and make
Sure that we wouldn't copy their mistake
Of neglecting our precious education
For some quick nine-to-five remuneration:
Though few of them had been given any real
Choice—straight out to work was the working-class deal.
　　　Just as our undisciplined waiting almost
Reached its silly farm antics limit, he burst
In through the door like a man on a mission,
With mortarboard in hand and black gown swishing.
Immediately labelled a total twat,
He resembled a bald, bespectacled bat,
But swiftly secured a ripple of applause
By matching his bake to back end of a bus,
While claiming he knew not what he was doing.
Despite the fact that most of us were pissing
Ourselves at the dishevelled get-up of him,
He got himself together, quietened the din,
Commanded the front, closed his eyes and opened
His mouth, and booklessly waved a verbal wand.
　　　He spoke of heartache, and numbness, and of pain;
Of what sounded like cold beer, good drugs, and wine;
Said stuff about dissolving, and forgetting,
In a place where there was no place for fretting ...
The very classroom walls seemed to draw their breath
When he talked of almost being in love with death.
　　　When teacher finished, he had no need to blush.
Coming round, out of the unreal teenage hush,
I turned and whispered to my mate beside me—
His mouth hanging open, his chin on his knee—
*Wow ... what does he call that thing when it's at home?*
*Not sure ... but I think he said it was a ... 'poem'?*
From that moment onward, there would be no doubt—
Liking poetry would be my 'coming out'.

# Sniper

God love the family from the Culmore Road
Who owned a huggable wee dog that they called
Sniper. *Sniper! Sniper!* they'd loudly sing-song.
At the time, Sniper could do no earthly wrong.
He was christened in the crisis produced by
Trigger-happy Paras on Bloody Sunday.
Then, the family had no hesitation
In calling him in from their Republican
Cul-de-sac of Derry's Catholic Culmore.
Indeed, they'd volunteer to stand at the door
In full public view to summon the Sniper.
They hollered his name with parade ground power
And Sniper would hear and scamper homewards
To be showered with head pats and big belly rubs.
　　　　Right up and through the years of the hunger deaths
They polished the medals on his doggy chest.
But even the Troubles couldn't hold its heat.
When sectarian tides began to retreat
Certain things became decidedly dodgy
As the area became more upwardly
Mobile. Mixed middle-class families began
To settle into Sniper's Culmore kingdom,
Bringing pedigree hounds out onto the grounds
To help harry the postmen on postal rounds.
Gradually, his owners grew shy to call
Sniper in by name. Tactfully, it was all
About playing to their prosperous neighbours
And 'Sniper' sounded classless to monied ears.
　　　　Sniper? Sniper? What on earth had possessed them?
As good Catholics, could they live down the shame?
Every time they had to call the dog in,
They would cup their mouths, whisper his name like sin,
Repeating *Sniper, Sniper, here boy, come here.*
And knowing no better, he'd always appear.
Caught in the cross-sights of respectable types,
Target of stares across avenues and drives,
In danger of lowering the area's
Tone, cutting the price tag on their new neighbour's

Homes, they couldn't be guilty of such a thing
In a community where money was king.
Did Sniper feel rejected? Did he feel blue?
Think why weren't they hollering like they used to?
Maybe he mused as he came in off the streets
On why whispered calls came with more doggy treats.
        But if this teaches anything of value—
Naming in anger can come back to bite you—
Today, it need hardly be said, that you need
A dog called Sniper like a hole in the head.

# Flags

*Flags, fucking flags …*
*What real use have they ever been to anyone?*
*Oh yeah, we've marched behind them*
*Plenty of times, but save to wrap our proud*
*Big-bellied patriotic selves up in, what else?*
*Waste of fucking time, waste of fucking cloth,*
*If you ask me …*

Raised with the results of patriot bragging,
I have always been wary of flag-waving.
Going into an American classroom
To talk to some children about where I'm from,
I notice the Irish tricolour hanging
Print-new and proudly from the classroom ceiling.
It's natural to assume I'm from Ireland.
How do I explain about Northern Ireland?
As a holder of both passports from back home
(Dissenting attempt to annoy everyone)
I am determined to keep my big mouth stum.
Why bother splitting history hairs with children?
But soon as the beaming teacher stretches out
Her hand in confident welcome, I blurt out
That the flag isn't the flag of my country.
At first she thinks that I'm just being funny,
But I gently insist that the flag is wrong.
Befuddled embarrassment, agitation,
Summarises the look on the teacher's face,
But I tactfully stress that if I'm to teach
The children, accurately, about where I'm from,
She'll have to accept that the flag is … well … wrong.
            To put things, technically, on the right track
I say that the flag should be the Union Jack.
Seeing another huge question mark take her face,
I speak of the red, white and blue, the British
Flag of T-shirt fame, of Buckingham Palace,
And suddenly she's back in her happy place,
Promising me that the Union Jack will soon
Be flying in full glory in the classroom.
I feel guilty, worried about the hassle,
The expense, but she sees it's a teachable
Moment and reassures me that it's okay.

I return to the school the very next day
To find the mischief-makers hung side by side.
It then becomes clear I've still got to decide
How to fairly present wee Northern Ireland
Without draping another flag beside them—
The red-handed standard of the Ulstermen.
Feels ridiculous making the suggestion,
But poor teacher runs with it, claiming it shall
Be no problem swinging a third flag at all.
        On my last visit, just a few days later,
There hangs the full blood-handed flag of Ulster,
Centre stage in the troublesome trinity:
Perfectly appropriate, it seems to me,
Given Ulster's piggy-in-the-middleness
From one British-Irish conflict to the next.
The flags are my visual three point sermon
As I attempt to educate the children.
Who's to know if anything makes sense to them?
If not, it isn't for the want of trying.
        I joke on the phone with a friend back home
That the flags are eenie meenie miney, min-
Us moe. He laughs, but tells me I'm getting slow
If I think I can get away without moe.
There's a fourth flag needed for the equation
To list all the flags of the Ulster Question.
I have forgotten the nine county, not six,
Version of Ulster's banner—red hand, red cross
Set against a bright yellow, not white, background—
A flag fit for flying in Donegal Town.
Tempted to further enlighten the teacher,
I've a hunch my messages mightn't reach her.

*Our mutual sectarian alchemies,*
*Which changed green, white and orange*
*Into green, white and gold,*
*Made real political progress seem*
*As elusive as the old philosopher's stone.*
*Sure it would've been easier to find a fart*
*In a field of flags, fart-flapping*
*On a blustery Ulster morning, than to imagine*
*Us ending up with 'The Chuckle Brothers'.*

# Budgie

*Drive the Demon of Bigotry home to his den,*
*And where Britain made brutes, now let Erin make men!*
—from 'Erin' by William Drennan (1754-1820)

It seemed like every single house had one
Except us, though we had an aquarium,
The other housed comfort of the working class,
One behind the bars, the other behind glass.
I thought it odd that the underprivileged
Would happily keep something tanked or caged,
Considering our hard human condition.
I guessed it was our identification
With creatures as poorly predestined as we
Often believed our hand-to-mouth selves to be.
Keeping birds in seed is a real kind of love,
And sprinkling fish-flakes like manna from above.
            Now by a strange quirk of imagination—
Some new light from within, something gene-given—
Every time I saw a map of Ireland
I rebelled against the usual notion,
The bird's-eye, map-driven visualisation
Of Ireland backed to the masculine mainland,
Her leafy petticoats eyed-up for stripping,
Her feminine fields ripe for penile ploughing.
Even as a child, I refused to see it
As a victim, back-turned towards Brit-
Ain, inviting colonial rear-ending.
*I* saw it as a battling budgie, facing
The mainland, proudly, prepared for what might come
Winging over the waves from the gauntlet realm.
Though couched by Drennan to properly provoke
His fellow Irishmen to throw off the yoke,
It was no 'base posterior of the world',
Arsehole waiting to be slavishly buggered
By a foreign foe even our side flinched at.
No more servile hung'ring for the 'lazy root',
But male and broad-shouldered as The Hill of Caves—
Where the United Irishmen first swore slaves
Would be set free by jointly overturning
The home-based kingdom of the sectarian—
Our bold-hearted budgie had come of age,
Had climbed the ladders and looked in the mirrors,

Then ignored the dudgeon doors and bent the bars,
Self-paroled, assuming independent airs.
        So turned towards the royal raven of England,
To my mind, our Irish budgie was crowned
With the head of Ulster: the tufty hair of
Wind-blown Donegal, the brawn and brains of
Radical Belfast, the 'Athens of the North',
With the clear blue eye of Neagh, and beak of Ards,
Heart, lungs and Dublin barrel-bulge of Leinster,
The fiery feet and claws of mighty Munster,
And thrown-back western wings of mystic Connaught.
Four provinces, four-square, forever landlocked,
Friend of brother Celts, but full of righteous rage
Against the keeper of the keys to the cage,
The Bard's 'blessed plot', his 'precious stone set in
The silver sea', his 'dear, dear land', his England.
Yes, no Catholic cage, nor Protestant pound,
Could hold my dissenting ideal of Ireland.
For in spite of spite, it was Drennan's Eden,
'In the ring of this world the most precious stone!'
His 'Emerald of Europe', his 'Emerald Isle'
Which no vengefulness would finally defile.

*Hickory Station*

# The Poetry Porch

*for Molly & Micah*

My driver's window is open to the world
As I sit at the fumy crossroads waiting
For the lights to shift from red to green.
A loud crack sets off a car alarm behind
Me in the car park of Lowes. The thunder
Thief is back. Sky shoulders boast black cloud

Epaulettes. Weather wars are about to blow.
It seems like the lights are stuck on red,
In league with the angry god above.
I'm sinking in the humid heat, when my eye's
Taken by a white cherry blossom by
The roadside, celebrating in the frisky wind,

Shedding party petals like there's no tomorrow.
The Japanese know them as flowers of death,
Living and dying in a blinding show.
I am grateful for the persistence of
Whiteness in the sunless dark, as they pepper
The Blazer with their papery buckshot.

Just as I'm about to put up the window,
Just as things are about to change from stop to go,
A single blossom comes straight for me and
Lands a soft, pure touch on my Irish nose.
So, I carry its white kiss home and pass it on,
To you, through this page from the poetry porch.

# Breath

What is death,
but a letting go
of breath?

One of the last
things he did
was to blow up

the children's balloons
for the birthday party,
joking and mock-cursing

as he struggled
to tie all
those futtery teats.

Then he flicked them
into the air
for the children

to fight over.
Some of them
survived the party,

and were still there
after the funeral,
in every room of the house,

bobbing around
mockingly
in the least draft.

She thought about
murdering them
with her sharpest knife,

each loud pop
an angry bullet
from her heart.

Instead, in the quietness
that followed her
children's sleep,

she patiently gathered
them all up,
slowly undoing

each raggedy nipple,
and, one by one, she took his
last breaths into her mouth.

What is life,
but a drawing in
of breath?

# Without Warning

Comes on without warning, the ache of Eden,
That soul-longing for the wholeness we all lack.

It may be no more than a learned delusion,
Or evidence of something we will win back.

# Mercy

Back from the community
college and haunted
by the face of the young
boy with siblings in tow,

walking the roadside dirt
in the sulphurous heat,
manfully struggling
to shepherd them home,

worry filling his face
looking towards the adults
haunting the rundown
porch he's headed for.

O Lord, Most High,
have mercy on our souls,
for the Kingdom of Heaven
is surely his!

# The Hanging Heart Chart

of evening's anatomy

is not as black
as the truest Blues

but washed with Burton's
white melancholy

being somewhere between
those pillared extremes

of sure-I-never-knew-ya
and deep topophilia

while the disembodied
voice announcing

the football fortunes
of the Red Tornadoes

comes and goes like bad
reception on mountain radios

and the dogs are crowing
and the birds are clicking

their fingers and thumbs
and cicadas are background

radiation from some big bang
and rose bulbs need changing

and house lights are too bright
and cars fly by too loud and too fast

and there's Einstein riding
bitch, smiling, like

he knows what IT means
and I gotta get outta my house

pants and into my jeans
and someone has touched down

'cause I can hear the screams

# For Us to Share

I get to walk my son to school and back
each weekday, weather permitting, and each

day, on our way home, he stops to select
a leaf and a tree nut, the fallen kind

that drop on sidewalks and parked cars this time
of year, and I urge him to go gentle

with the leaf, and he always asks me, *Why?*
I say, it's beautiful, but it's brittle,

and easily destroyed. So he carries
it home each day like it is the last leaf

left for us to share in the whole wide world.

# Song

I was close to sawing
some leafless limbs

from the dogwood tree
when, right on cue,

a robust robin
appeared on one

and sent its soul out
across the lawn.

So, I let them be,
since even a barren

bough can hold a song.

# Wordless

*for Molly*

I know we were
on a great day out,
and only parting
for an agreed
hour or two,
but I would rather,
really, have stayed
with you and him,
to watch you
shoot pinball together

in the Asheville arcade,
than to be rolling down
Walnut Street, fancy free,
on my way to graze
in Downtown Books,
and onwards to curry
our carryout from
marvellous Mela ...
for I didn't like
the sudden feeling

that I was already gone,
and that you two,
so much younger,
were the only family left ...
it's true, that even
for the likes of me,
a relentless word-hoarder,
that sometimes books
don't matter a damn.
So, love, I want

you to know,
that when it comes
to you and him—
like when you first

slid your hand
inside my jacket
and laid it on
my racing heart—
that wordless is still
the favoured flame.

# Worthy

Caught without proper paper,
I'm writing this on the back
of my son's Air Blasters gun
cardboard packaging won from
the Carolina Beach Arcade,

while sitting on the Hurricane
Bar rooftop, with a view
of the amusements on one side,
the Atlantic on the other,
and a supermoon in the sky

being snapped by the many
with their adult pacifiers.
Writing about looking down
on the boardwalk Putt-Putt course
at two males proudly adorned

with matching tacky Stetsons,
and sporting, even more proudly,
matching rebel flag T-Shirts,
their kids noticeably punching
the air with their fists as they

celebrate each ugly bogey.
Writing about my eye then catching
sight of a wonderfully built
black man walking past Putt-Putt
with a serene smile on his face,

and wearing a T-shirt with
the one word slogan—'WORTHY'.
Overhead, as I pay my tab,
pelicans patrol the promenade with
something still approaching innocence.

# Knowledge

Sometimes we can lose
those closest to us
not to death
but to life
to a project that
doesn't include us in it
(well, maybe, not enough)

to a room inside the other
that only they can enter
to a life that has
ten thousand things
with them only at its centre
to a country that simply
is too far for us

to ever visit ever
to another person
another love
that deserves
all their attention
Sometimes it's simply
like that

though it's seldom
ever simple
but for our own
heart's sake
let us determine
that such knowledge
is somehow ample

# Grief

Calling repeatedly
for an absent mate,

a single red bird will
be autumn's last leaf.

# Sometimes I Think

Sometimes I think that my happiest days
Have been spent in bookshops;
Especially when everything's in bloom,

When the trees have hung out
Their flags on every street,
And the clouds have gone AWOL

Or been safely penned
By that orange collie of the skies:
It's then that I'm in my element

Because, because there's magic in the book.
Even Hewitt, custodian of reason,
Was moved to heresy as he took me

By the elbow in his house
To tour his library, his working collection,
And pointed to a buckramed book

On the jam-packed shelves. *See this one?*
*Believe it or not, and I sense you will,*
*Roberta and I were in Edinburgh,*

*And as we hurried past a second-hand*
*Bookshop, I suddenly stopped and said*
*That I needed, quickly, to go in.*

*I knew, somehow I just knew,*
*That there was a book on the shelf*
*That was somehow meant for me.*

*So we entered, and I went straight*
*To it, reached for it, and took it.*
*Now, that's all that I can tell you.*

*It was there. And it was for me.*
My friend always says that we should
Choose our addictions well.

I think I have. Only time will tell.

# Heavy

sunset
diluting
orange

moonrise
cuff-linked
chaperone

sibling
of our seething star
crooning

O
heavy
is
the
world
for
those
who
bear
its
weight

# Advice to a Young Poet

If you've any
ambition,
lose it early.

For what's
ambition worth,
if you're here

to tell the truth?

# To Memorise

*after MR*

Before heading to bed,
Before cancelling
The back room light,

Too tired to play pick up,
I take a long look at the path
I must take across the floor

Through my son's toy debris
And into the hallway
(Adorned, would you believe,

With the same floral wallpaper
Of my grandparents' hallway
In the home where I started).

I close my eyes to memorise
My whereabouts in the certain
Dark. Then set out.

# Little Things

Sometimes things seem a little less lonely,
Turning my eyes to the starry prairie,

Seeing the old familiar Plough still there,
Part of my America. Only here

Folk have always known it as the Big Dipper,
And that makes things even lonelier.

# Harold

*in memory of H. T. Roddy (1924–2013)*

It's Gastonia, and it's Sunday.
Raindrops crater the windscreen.
Sirens moan like mating cats.
Things are rundown and rained on.
Like parts of Belfast, but with heat.

We squeak into the car park
Of the Brian Center for Care
To take our chances with Granddaddy.
Conifers umbrella the car,
Saving us from a downpour.

We get out and go in. It's like
Casting a full-blown scene from
'The Regions of Sin':
Immobiles like blanched whales;
People with barely enough skin

To cover the bone; long-life lifers,
Diabetes-deformed; lung-challenged
Old folk, still cancer-sticked,
Chair-free at the Care Center door.
We know the room we are looking for.

We hold our breath, smile the corridor,
Almost hold our noses, too.
We reach his room, double-check,
Then dander in all bonhomie,
Hoping Harold knows it's we.

Husband, truck driver, card-shark, Granddaddy!
Sit up in bed and tell us the score!
Sometimes it's surprisingly good, like normal:
Others, it's playing tigtag with the past,
Unsure how long each memory will last.

But Molly loves to go with him,
Milk every word for all it is worth;

Even when something sounds hurtful,
Every exchange is ladled with love.
Memory at all is song of the dove.

Harold, I cherish the days I sat on the sofa
Across from your big chair in the trailer
And chewed the fat over Tiger and Phil
Or Junior and Tony and The Intimidator—
My American 'Billy' and me in front of TV.

Now you seem to remember very little.
Or is it everything?  Sundowners
Dawns on you every time the disc drops.
Dementia's the word on no one's lips.
Our loving family trinity,

Marylou and Molly and Michelle,
Will see you through until the end,
Then carry your ashes to the wished-for sea:
The sea I'm glad that I crossed over to find
Your granddaughter, and to be your friend.

# Soundside

*for Mary Rowe*

Suitably emerald wetlands;
Young crows in the crows' nests
Of earthed aerials strung

Like some old ship's rigging;
High-flown jets and speedboats
Zooming their frothy contrails;

Cloud choirs congregating
To lead the evening worship
Of water, the primal parent.

Top-decked, up with the tree-sway,
Bird-eyed, dove-call comforted,
My chosen tablets are *Self-Reliance*,

*High Lonesome* and *Parnassus* from
The bookshelf lucky bags of home.
This is the spot where the sun sets,

The soundside, paradoxically silent,
Holding its lake-like own against
The seaside's surfable commotion;

So quiet I can almost hear the well-wish
The sun makes as it drops into the beyond.
Now to sit, caberneted, to watch supermoon

Build a Stonehenge of shadow until dawn.

# The Great Table

In the silent semi-dark,
while working at the words,
I reached to backhand-brush

what I thought were cookie
crumbs from the cover of
*Faithful and Virtuous Night*

by the poet Louise Glück,
and was startled to realise
that I was trying to erase

the stars of The Milky Way
from the cover photograph.
One day, perhaps, that's how

the Maker will clean off
those cosmic crumbs from
the great table of the Universe.

# Recognition

The buds are beginning to open,
the young leaves are on their way.
Soon they'll be giving me
their green full-handed waves.
I would love to just stand here
at this upstairs window

and watch them as they grow.
But I know, even if I stood here
for a full day, without blinking,
I would still miss everything,
I would still not be a party
to their supernatural way.

Which makes me remember
that's how life always is.
We don't notice people growing
when we're travelling with them.
It's only separation which lends
recognition, the shock of decay.

The deal-with-the-devil of the émigré.

# Hickory Haiku

*for Chrisanne and Lamar*
*& Georgia and Stewart*

*Providing a home*
*from home—our necessary,*
*neighbourly angels.*

I

Fiftieth birthday:
musings between here and there,
there and back again.

II

We Irish aren't wooed
by weather: but, for folk here,
it's a love affair.

V

Sam's Club girl shakes my
hand, says: *You're the first Ireland*
*that I've ever met!*

VI

Valley Hills shopping
mall: women wear their new-found
breasts like 1st rosettes.

VIII

Night-winds lay the corn
rows low. Morning, they rise—
foals finding their feet.

XI

Full-faced moon-gazing ...
I love how s/he dwells in
approachable light.

XII

Carolina Beach:
moonlit beer-caps on midnight
sand—redneck sea-shells!

XVII

Our mountain wedding—
the wind rose, filling the sails
of our holy vows.

XIX

The sun's done gone. Dark
ink surges through sky water—
a storm's a-comin'!

XXI

Tombstones in front yards:
bodies hung from trees—Hallo'
ween in Hickory!

XXII

O elderly moon,
a lidless eye blurred by a
cloudy cataract.

XXIII

Camel crickets rest
on the dusty, starlit floor
like lunar modules.

## XXIV

Invading our space,
carpenter bees hover—come
and go. UFOs!

## XXXI

I feel good, I knew
that I would, now to have a
first dream in colour.

## XXXII

Belfast storage has
arrived! I swerve and swoop, book-
to-book, swallow-eyed.

## XXXIV

There is always one
dog that barks a background to
the birdsong of thought.

## XXXVI

Bittersweet pillars
of melancholy: holy
opportunities.

## XXXVII

Cell phones are legion—
techno mobiles hung over
our modern mangers.

XL

Same the world over—
the smug freemasonry of
the mediocre.

XLI

Out of work ...... means play ...
means thoughts ... means words ... means play with
words ... means poems ...... means work!

XLII

We whinny and neigh,
two rocking horses grazing
the pasture of porch.

XLIV

Night trains clippety-
clop through downtown Hickory—
The Tornado Trot.

XLV

Nature's risky here.
Nothing's poisonous back home ...
except some people.

XLIX

Cemetery short-
cut ... the otherworldly weight
of that strange estate.

# Dominion

Just as easily, I could
have elected to sit
in the half-lit
downtown tavern,
or lounge in the soft sofa
wine shop on the square,
conscience polar clear,
being blessed by
my working wife,
busy putting her players
through their pre-*Antigone*
agonies at the Tractor Shed Theatre;
but I chose, instead, to perch,
once again, on the porch,
among the happy families
of robins and blue jays,
cardinals and doves,
listening to their necessary
chitterings; soaking in
the stoic wisdom
of trees and shrubs.
And then I realised,
like for the first real time,
that they are all in our care—
all in our care—
and that dark word
came back to rock
me in my chair.

# Hidden

I have always had one foot
in the field, the other on the street,
so the front door balcony's

a happy halfway house for me,
a redeemable version
of being hidden in plain sight.

Tonight, I have wallowed
in the aerial acrobats,
those silent criss-crossers,

crazy loop-lappers, gobs full of bugs.
And now I'm noticing how
the bright roses are suddenly

turned off at sundown,
even before the soft light
is up, leaving everything green

to be more than seen, to be felt.
I know that we need sunlight
to prosper, but we dare not

neglect the benefits of dusk,
when the moon lies its lovely, tilted
head down on the night's blue bed.

# Open Space

Unusually, the avenue's full of children,
Racing here and there with happy screams.
I'll just sit tight. Soon they'll be drawn
Inside to supper in front of screens.

And when they are, the avenue's fuller
Now that it's almost empty, now that there's
Only the inplaceness of curtained houses
And the silent patience of planted things.

I love this porch, this open space, this
Rented window on the world. Candle flames
Flicker in the faintest wind, side-stepping
Their reflections in their pools of wax.

'Meet me at the corner where two trees meet'
Is the given line that's keeping me taxed.
As darkness rises, I suddenly imagine
Myself gluing fireflies to my fingers for light.

# Hobo

*for Kevin Todd*

So buried in a book
I almost missed them

But I looked up
Just in time to see

Two classic lines of sunlight
Tracking our neighbour's yard

And how the hobo in me
Ran to jump the train

That rode such rails
Just as they disappeared

# Nature

*Nature never wears a mean appearance.*
    —Ralph Waldo Emerson, 'On Nature'

Just when you think
you have clinched the deal
on that certain equilibrium
which some of us mere mortals
seem doomed to seek—
sitting in the porch-shade
on a steamy afternoon,
with the wee man sat happily
in his garden sandbox—
a big bumblebee steers
straight for you at an unnatural
speed, and then won't go away.
So, you find yourself belting
it irritably out of your porch-space
with the full-handed back
of a Bill Stafford poetry book—
an exemplary pacifist—
to the old Belfast tune of
*Get the hell out of here!*
Blushing, flustered, you then
return to the book,
feeling silly, a little guilty,
certainly less than mature,
back to that elusive goal
of being fully one with other
humans, and with nature.

# This Far

The evening avenue is psalmist-still.
There's not one single breath of breeze
To trouble the tall sails of the trees.

The main road is now the main deck,
And the porch is a hung-up lifeboat
For the mind, and the body, and soul.

Everything else rooted is peculiarly calm:
Each blade of grass, each honeysuckle,
Each molten-marvellous garden rose.

The only things which are still moving
Are the bugs and birds, and all those
Rolling by in the huff and puff

Of passing cars. With my welcome wife,
And my youngest son, I am content to be,
So to speak, so completely lost at sea

On yet another liquid lap around our
Mid-life star. And I am constantly
Grateful to have ever come this far.

# The Electric Life

*The transaction that we call the experience of poetry
always takes place between one being and another.
The energy circulates from privacy to privacy.*
    —Sven Birkerts, 'The Electric Life'

Night after night,
I feared they'd left me,
decided to drop me
like an old flame.
Each evening, near dusk,
their courting time,
I studied the tall trees
outlined like coastlines
against the blue,
their blue gaps
like lakes or loughs,
and waited. But nothing.

Then, the other evening,
I saw something
in the treetops,
not golden-green
but white light,
blinking on and off,
that I mistook for planes,
but which was them.
Were they starting
in the heavens,
where they normally finish,
and working down?
Or were they simply
being newborn?
They were still
so much better
than the predicted
meteor shower,
being living light,
not inanimate matter
borrowing fire from
our atmosphere.

And then, tonight,
while I'm glowing
with Birkerts' book,
they've returned,
in all their glory, playing
peek-a-boo with my eyes,
so many of them sailing
slowly around the porch
like gentle Zeppelins,
close enough to touch.
This is the life.
The real electric life.

# Just

Just rained for all
of fifteen seconds,

something sudden
arriving from

somewhere else,
bringing sound

with its wetness.
Never known it

to rain so little,
so drop and go:

like dribbles from
incontinent clouds,

or lippy overflows
from brimming

sky-baths, whose taps
have been turned off,

just in time.

# The Old Trees

*Like dolmens round my childhood, the old people.*
—John Montague

Like dolmens round our houses, the old trees,
Each rooted to a designated spot;
None of them holding any real aces,
With birthplace, and graveyard, dealt out by rote.
Yes, it's here that they'll have to live, and die,
And nowhere else. Yet they own the 'profound'—
That being silently satisfied with one's life.
Fully clothed, or naked, they stand their ground.
Patient circle of leaf leviathans—
Who only wave their skyward tails in storms
When the clouds burst, and the winds have risen,
And the air is thick with floodable rain—
They stay strong through moving generations,
And none of them ever seem to complain.

# Wasps

On an unseasonably
warm afternoon
I am back on the porch,
and the little wasps
are trying to build
in the hollow arms and legs
of my aluminium chair.

They're determined,
as they are every spring,
to inhabit my chosen seat,
but I have soaked
their sought-for portals
with gasoline, being equally
determined to stay put.

But on they come,
at regular intervals,
in ones and twos only,
as if one sometimes needs
the second as witness to carry
the story of occupation back
to the others, to be believed.

I wonder what they think of me,
and feel sorry for them,
almost guilty, even imagining
the dark openings they seek
as being cave mouths
in which they wish to store
some valuable scrolls.

So I am kind to myself,
reminding myself

that it's my chair, my porch,
though I can hear them protesting
*But we were here first!*
Fair enough. But no matter.
For I have a porch thirst.

Gasoline will win the day,
for another year, anyway,
and I will sit safely and securely
behind my slatted battlements,
scratching the pale page
hoping, as always, to be
stung by poetry.

# Zapper

*for Paul Durcan*

Almost couchant on the porch,
goggling the eye-candy
of our freshly mown yard,
fighting the thought
that so many of my favourite
things are no more than
professional killing machines,
when a gentle garden redcoat
does some floppy mid-air karate
to take down an ambling bug.

As I instinctively avert my gaze,
swivelling the periscope of my showered
head, a ginger tabby pads its way
onto the road and hunkers down,
tail slowly sweeping the sun-warmed tarmac,
eyes lasering in on another robin
plying its own murderous trade
on the cleanly shaven lawn.
And so I rise up to scupper
the tabby's deadly intent.

But then comes the first ever
avenue sound of a bug zapper!
Least that's what I'm calling it,
for now; a phosphorescent slab of light,
luminating near the garage doors
of the old Marine's house opposite:
a sinister contraption, a perilous attraction,
reminiscent of Kubrick's obelisk
that so enchanted chimps. This one
fries every bug that gravitates too close.
A white hole, if I've ever seen one.
It's a killing ground over there.
A perpetual evening electric chair.

Sometimes, Paul, it's all too hard to thole—
almost enough to drive one to thon crystal meth—
that in the midst of this silver sliver of life,
we are always so much in league with death.

# Everything Is Going to Be All Right

*for Derek Mahon*

The mountains are wearing grey wigs.
Rain clouds are hanging their drapes.
Down here, it's hot and dry.
Cicadas are back.
Night-waves for the land-locked.

I'm Piedmont-porched.
I've been away for a few days,
Head-down in the books,
Wrestling with Morgan's
'Interests, Conflict, and Power'.

(An American comma
After 'Conflict'—not ours.)
But now I'm back on the street.
Back at the real work. The poesy.
A couple of nights ago,

A bubble-blow of fireflies
Meteored my study window,
As if they were signalling me
To come out to play—like we
Did with wee torches in our day—

As if they had missed me as much
As I had missed them.
And now, tonight, they're putting on
A display. Some of them even
Rounding the porch like they're

Anointing it with light ......
Everything is going to be all right.

# Hoover

A late night car zooms
in with blaring lights,
like the old Hoover
my granny pushed

across the carpeted floors
of her timber home,
driving me into corners
where I didn't want to go,

but which I knew were
safe, because I knew
that she was always
on my side despite how

it might seem otherwise.
In fond memory of her,
I still feel safe in those scary
places where I go to hide.

# A Dream of Home

A white shirt pegged
to the old clothesline
out the back of our house
on Derrycoole Way

was flip-flopping
in the summer wind
when it changed into
a perfect white swan

which I somehow
captured and ferried
back into the living room
of our house

where it perched upon
the low lake of the window-
ledge and sat there staring
at the passing people

# Debt

Like when the wind and rain come
for you, slapping you about the bake,
and your tired-out mother,
in her heavy collared coat,
loaded down with shopping bags,
white-knuckled hands near numb,
steps in front to take the brunt,

then stops as the gale gets worse,
turning her back to the lashing
romper-rooming your skinny bones,
and opens her sodden coat to spread
round you and your younger brother
sitting chap-cheeked in the toy-like tansad
you're struggling to wheel him in.

# The Milky Way Café

In Belfast, back in the day,
My mother carried a bomb

Out of The Milky Way Café,
And calmly set it down

In the middle of the path
Opposite The Belfast Telegraph.

It was destroyed by the army.
When the media asked

Just what had possessed
Her, she quickly replied:

*Possessed whom?*

# The Apologist

Fine words from a man
From whom words come easily—
Drawn from his midnight mouth
Like a chain of silken scarves.

# Sigh

I sigh a lot now.
I never used to,
But I do.

I sigh for myself,
I know,
But I also sigh

For you.

# Distance

Sometimes
most times

the distance
is too far

Like trying
to touch

your own face
in the mirror

# The Right Word

*for Larry Monteith*

*Put your ears to the trees ... what can you hear?*
Children and teachers move in to listen,
Touching each trunk like there's something to fear,
Their faces full of anticipation.
Then the shock as everyone fathoms
The hidden melody of living trees,
That sounds like they hold tremendous gallons
Thundering into invisible seas.
Both teachers and children gather themselves
To pen a few words to frame for the shelves
And walls of their classrooms and families.
One tough guy checks it was water he heard—
*Same water that rolls through you and through me—*
Then moves on, chuffed that he knew the right word.

# Related

*for Brian Murphy (1949–2014)*

'Thran'—
A classic Ulsterism:
Stubborn, contrary, cross-grained.

Personally, I'm convinced
It comes from 'Thracian'—
A Roman racehorse,

Untouchable, barbarian.
True or false, there's me,
Standing at a bar toilet-trough

In rural Mullaghbawn,
Lined up alongside a posse
Of smiling old men:

*We believe you're related to*
*Our big man?*

I am.

*That's good, that's good …*
*Though I trust you're not as ……*

Thran?

# The Other Side

*for Matthew Rice (1906–1964)*

Scanning my Catholic
granda's Mass card,
suddenly death
seems more exciting,
the natural next step.

*We have loved him in life, let us*
*Not forget him in death.*

From St. Ambrose,
who lay in his cradle
dribbled with honey
from bees who had
blessed him with
their liquid gold,
giving his father
some high hopes
for his eloquence
and honeyed tongue.

Then there's 'Ambrosia',
the nectar of the gods.
And then there's
'Ambrosia Creamed Rice',
the tinned working-class dish
we had to enjoy—urban
frogspawn, the cheap clotted
water of working-class life.

*We have loved him in life, let us*
*Not forget him in death.*

And let us not forget the storm and the strife.

# The Fated Hour

*for Kenneth Robert Rice (1938–2014)*

> *Thou hast felt*
> *What 'tis to die and live again before*
> *Thy fated hour.*
> —John Keats, 'Hyperion: A Vision'

Over my father
Hangs
The fated hour.

I know that I
Will be unable
To proffer proper

Consolation,
In person, but
I am trying, vainly,

To hold his hand
By phone;
A hand as once

As squat
And four-square
As my very own:

Palm-proud,
Knuckle-bright,
Fist-sure—

The hand
He gave me
When I was born.

And gave me,
As a child,
When I would fall.

A hand that was also
Too ready, on occasion,
To set me straight;

The same hand that
Kept me from harm.
For 'One Punch Ken'

Was nobody's doll,
Even in Rathcoole.
Hurt me, hurt us,

You hurt all.
Comforting cliché,
I see him in the mirror,

And feel him in my hand.
Psalmist! Oul Psalmist!
Everything now is

That old sinking sand.

*New Poems*

# With Everything

*for Matthew*

Like all good clichés,
the comic strip scenario's true—
kids fleeing from an angry adult
whose window has been smithereened
by a duffed attempt at goal.

But that shot was often
the one with the biggest dream
of Wembley glory behind it,
the all or nothing try
to ripple the old onion bag

and bring thousands to their feet.
This morning, the local pool
is window-flat. It's all I can do
to stop myself from climbing the fence
to break it with my body,

with everything I've got.

# Because

*for Charis & Pip*

She reached
her hand out
to her lover

on a quiet evening
in a quiet moment
when everything

just seemed to
make so much sense
and it wasn't just

her own hand
but the hand
of all of us. And

everything seemed
suddenly possible
because it was

# Darling

*in memory of John Montague*

Not that any of us needed
to hear any more of it,
in an awful year full

of significant leave-takings,
but we garnered the news
on gorgeous Sanibel Island,

the very day we'd set aside
to dander the wildlife refuge
that is "Ding" Darling.

And what a place it is,
brimming with wildlife
being watched and photographed

mainly by those running high
on rich retirement dollars,
while running low on life.

We left nothing but footprints,
took nothing but pictures.
And we couldn't help but think

that though they weren't
our native, freshwater trout,
that the mullets, all "tendril-light"

in the lazy swamps, looked like
fish you'd love to guddle.
They were gathering in their

fluid cathedrals just for you, John—
O "bodiless lord of creation"—
just waiting for your caging touch.

# Captiva

*for Woody & Dorothy*

Late afternoon, and shiny dolphins
ring-bind the shoreline
as another Floridian folder
is about to close; story of those
who scribble the sea-page
with their yachts and boats.
On medallioned marinas
they catch the last of the rays,
sipping martinis in the heavenly
sunset of their lives.
Here, death is an offense—
the gate-crashing gigolo
who wanders in and out

of palm-rich driveways
with a silent scythe;
the old killjoy that should
be ashamed to show
its party-pooping face
on such a happy shore.
But it wasn't always so.
Not when 'Gasparilla',
'last of the Buccaneers',
ran the eastern Gulf like a
card-shark at his own casino;
hoarding concubines on Captiva;
giving the island its name.

Cannonballed by an American
schooner, they say he greeted
death with a cheer, winding a
chain around his waist and
sinking like an anchor.
Some nights, from private docks,
the people of Captiva

can still hear his last cry
troubling the breeze;
and hear his chains
sounding from the deep
in the rattle of their ice cubes,
and the clink of each glass.

# Time

*Our bodies, someday,*
*Will have to wear stone.*
  —Larry Levis, 'Those Graves in Rome'

Time, that old artiste,
loosens the canvas

which was stretched
across us

when we were born;
slackens the skin

on our face, on our bones,
preparing us

for the final roll-up
of our days,

when it will store us
in the cold drawers

of the earth.

# Given

*for Melanie Ward*


It was okay as long
as I stayed away, but going back
has got me well off track,

the landscape of home
shocking the old heart
back into its native rhythm.

Standing outside Limepark,
unpacking the car in
the country dark,

drinking in the heavens,
with the Plough hung
smack overhead,

I stopped to give
thanks for seeing it
again in an Antrim sky,

its bullet points
as clear as day ...
when a shooting star

came and went across
the homely constellation.
So I stood, rooted,

watching the sky for another
thirty minutes or more,
waiting on a meteor shower,

almost refusing to believe
that just one timely
arc would be given.

# Cold Comforts

The summer morning YM crowd
had my head well deeved,
so I chose to trot around
the local graveyard instead,
and found right good company
among the avenued dead,
a foreign legion of surnames
from Ulster's smelting pot:

Anderson, Abernethy, Aitken,
Beattie, Blair, Ball, Burns and Black,
Caldwell, Collins, Gorman and Graham,
Wilson and Walker and Wright,
McCullough, McClure, Murphy and Todd,
Smith and Jones and Rose and Hill and Hone ...
to name but some of those
cold comforts from home.

# Sorrow-Songs

*for Martin Andrew Beattie (1958-2016)*

### I. See Your Face

I can still see your face
at the dining room window,
face almost against the glass,
a sad ghost of yourself.

You'd been grounded
by your loving mother
who'd togged you out
again in print-new clothes

from her Kay's Catalogue,
and had only let you out
on the promise that
you wouldn't come home dirty.

But she must have known.
You and I and a couple of mates
made our way up through the estate
to the foot of Carnmoney Hill,

to what we'd aptly named,
the 'muck hills'. Workmen
had been laying pipe for weeks,
and the rain had fashioned

a wide, waterlogged trench—
a leaping temptation
for someone as sporty as you.
So, we dared you to jump across

from one muddy bank to the other,
knowing, like you, what the result
would mean to your mother.
But you said it was no bother

and just took to the air.
You almost made it, but fell
heroically short, dragging your
fingertips down the farther bank

like a character from a classic cartoon.
We fished you out, holding back
the guilty laughs as best we could.
A drowned rat is what you looked like

as we walked you home.
We were next door neighbours,
so one by one friends dropped away,
and left us on our own at your front door:

you, to face the music;
me, to pray you'd be ok.
I missed playing with you that day,
more than I could ever properly say

for we were boys, mates, mini macho men.
Your mother hung your washed new clothes
on the backyard line, which drew me
out to look. They hung there,

empty of you, even your very gutties
pegged out to dry. That's when I
caught your windowed face, full of
longing for the world outside.

I wanted you to know, Marty,
that I wasn't laughing, that I was sad too,
and so I played out the back on my own.
And, like I'm doing now, once more,

I was waiting and watching for you to reappear.

II. Carnmoney

Marty, come back,
come back to me now,
and let's climb
the Carnmoney Hill
like we did
in the old days

(well, that's to say,
like we did
in our young days)
and let's go together
to 'The Well'
(to what, at least,

we called 'The Well',
an upright brick orifice
that leaked water
all year round,
hid in the low woods
above Fernagh,

our sister estate,
built after ours,
but with the same red brick)
and bring your Carnmoney-made
bow and arrows, and your
Gildea-bought Bowie

knife and sheath,
and let's go play
together, again,
for as long as you want,
at our childhood games
of life and death.

III. Dream Road

He came to me in a dream
two nights ago,
quicker than any of my dead
have ever come,
all freshly healthy,

beaming and gesturing
as we walked down a road
going from somewhere
to somewhere, together.
And as we were laughing

and bantering, as ever,
he put an arm around
my shoulder, looked me
in the face, smiled, and said,
*So, you're missing me then?*

I teared up, and so did he,
and then we walked on
down that dream road,
side by side, talking
and laughing as before.

# McNabney's

*for Barbara*

Flushed with some pocket money, we would dander
The Old Irish Highway to Cloughfern Corners
And along the Doagh Road to McNabney's shop.
You could buy almost anything there: top up
On basics like bread, and milk, and cigarettes,
Clear bags of sticks, firelighters, and peat briquettes.
But we coveted sweeties in big plastic
Jars: towering, lid-topped sentinels, standing like
Dolmens on some sugary Easter Island,
Shoulder-to-shoulder in ranked rows, and opened
At our command. Cola Cubes, Chocolate Éclairs,
Brandy Balls, Bon Bons, Cinnamon Lozenges,
Sherbet Strawberries, Apple Tarts, Murray Maids, all
Weighed on the scales and bagged at our beck-and-call.
We loved McNabney's on warm summer nights or
On cold winter ones with Christmas in the air.
But the main thing that stays in the memory
Is the image of the owner's daughter. She
Was always on duty, be it day or night.
Plainest Jane, certain spinster, nothing to write
Home about. She would ask, serve, take money, give
Change, all the while acting like we weren't alive.
She was the snigger-stock, the weirdo, the creep,
Who we'd only laugh at when back on the street.
But I was taken by her concentration,
Loved the way she ignored the situation
Caused by her staring out and above our heads.
I sensed she could see into all our lived lives.
If I could see her now, I would tell her that
She was right to so ignore us, right to strike
Out on her inward own, and fair play to her.
If I only knew her name, I would name her.

# The Silver Spoon

My father wasn't born with a silver spoon
In his mouth. Rather, he was transported soon
After his birth to a Home up in Belfast,
And there he stayed for five more years. His last
Day couldn't have come sooner—he was fostered
By Jimmy and Minnie Martin, who chauffeured
Him to Cambria Park, Whiteabbey, beside
Railway tracks that run from Belfast to seaside
Larne. He was foster-brother to two brothers:
Not mistreated, but nothing like those others,
As they were the apples of their parents' eyes.
In any day and age, sure that's no surprise.
      He grew up tough and he grew up mean, the boy
Named Sue had nothing on him: a nobody's
Fool, even if he was nobody's child. They
Sometimes had to send him home from school early
To protect kids from his fists. 'One Punch Ken' was
His young nickname, and it stuck, simply because
When he hit you, he hit you hard, and that meant
Lights out. For some, Ken sent home was heaven sent.
      But even now we've gone too far. We need to
Go back a bit, back before primary school,
Go back to the Home, back to his memory
Of a time when he was out on a sunny
Day in the grounds of the Home, when he was asked
To pay respects to a stranger who was whisked
Into his play. He always remembers her
As a lady, well dressed and well spoken, her
Demeanour immaculate, with a softish,
Kindly manner, with a man with an English
Accent. In dreams, he knows that she's his mother.
But what he remembers distinctly is more
Of the fear that she had come to confiscate
His spoon, his silver spoon, the spoon he would hate
To part with, the spoon which he played with in that
Playground dirt, the spoon he'd stolen off the bat.
But she was there, he'd felt her in ev'ry way.
Though she still remains a phantom to this day.

# Shimna

*for Damian Gorman*

She shimmies her way down through the forest,
shimmering here and there in sunlight or moonlight,

shivering in the rains, shaking under thunder,
playing peek-a-boo with lightning, her half-sister,

sliding over her riverbed and her river stones,
all that sunken sediment of the solid earth,

mirroring birds and branches and moody skies,
taking shadowy snapshots of us when we pass by,

showing nothing of herself, reflecting everything
that stoops to look into her see-through eyes,

everything that swoops and flickers across her
liquid lens, everything that plunges or suspends

itself in her, it's all recorded and downloaded
into the beautiful translucent file called Shimna.

# From Above

But a few hundred miles
from Earth,
our astronauts are missing
home so much

that they have tuned
all of their computers—
100 or more—
to a digital recording of

rain. Rain.
To a soundtrack of rain,
they are seven-dwarfing
their day away, ignoring

the terrors of rain, the boredom of rain,
being simply grateful for the comfort
falling into their ears, those
gentle droplets from

(what used to be) above,
so familiar, but now so strange,
a tippy-toe of teardrops from
beyond their present range ...

# On the Eve

Two thousand and fourteen,
you took my father. But tonight,
with that, I don't wish to go
any farther. I would much rather

consider these two big dogs
framed above the fancy urinal
of the champagne bookstore,
two well-groomed Alsatians

nuzzled together, cutely,
with the front one's tongue
lolling like a fine split ham.
The other is more aware than him,

more vigilant, though both dogs'
eyes are almost set the same.
They're staring at something
in the distance, maybe someone,

and they're on alert, as always,
but they share this perfectly
fearless affection, one's paw
placed snugly over the other's,

like there is nothing to fear.
But fear is what their casual
wariness is based on, it's what
makes them instinctively able

for their joint doggy futures.
I know that look well. Have seen
it in too many human eyes.
On the face of a mother. On her child's.

# Zulu

*for Annesley*

School was over.
The sun was shining.
Dad was home
from work, early.
Mum and dad
had smiling faces,
they beamed.
Dad laughed,
and joked,
and kissed Mum
lightly.
I was nine.
My brother
was six.
Dad surprisingly
suggested that
we should go
swimming,
my brother
and me.
He'd take us,
pay for us,
no problem.
Only nine, I knew
what he had
in mind.
But I agreed.
We loved to swim.
Mum waved us off,
worry-smiling.
It was thirty minutes
in the car
before we reached
the Grove Baths.
Unexpectedly,
the baths were shut.
Like a Sunday.
Dad cursed.

Hit the steering wheel.
Said fuck.
My brother and me
said, it's ok Dad.
He said fuck.
Then he said:
want to go
to the pictures?
My brother said no,
but I knew to say yes.
Dad smiled.
Slapped my thigh.
Turned the car around
and drove us back
to Rathcoole
to the Alpha cinema.
We got out,
wandered in.
I held my brother's hand.
All the movies
were too old for us.
But I agreed,
for my brother and me,
to watch *Zulu*.
Dad brought us extra
popcorn and treats,
everything we could ever need.
Then he left,
saying he'd be back
when the movie ended.
On the dot.
I knew he would be.
I took my brother's hand
and led us to a good seat
in the Alpha dark.
Soon after the adverts
and the roaring lion,
my brother

started crying.
We had our tight
swim trunks
under our shorts.
His were chapping him,
burning the inside
of his thighs.
I felt it, too.
So I took him
to the toilet,
told him to take
them off.
But he was just
too shy.
I led him back
to our seats.
Asked him, gently,
what he wanted us
to do.
He said he wanted
to go home.
But I knew what that
would bring.
He cried.
And apologised.
So I thought it through.
We left the expensive
popcorn and the treats
and the drinks.
I took him by the hand
out of the darkness
and into the light
of late afternoon.
He bore the chaffing
the whole way home,
from The Diamond
to Derrycoole Way.
When we reached

our front door,
he looked at me,
afraid. I took his hand,
rang the front doorbell.
We waited on hell.
Mum appeared
in her nightgown.
Looking sad,
she smiled, knelt down,
hugged us both.
Dad's bare legs
appeared at the top
of the stairs,
and we heard his
for fuck's sake!
What are they doing home?!
Mum begged him to stop, firmly.
She showed us into
our living room,
whispered to stay quiet,
promising that
all would be ok.
Ignoring the curses
from upstairs,
she fetched warm underwear
from the tumble dryer.
We changed quickly.
Then she took us
to the back door
and sent us out to play.
As we walked away,
the back door opened,
and I turned to hear
her say to make sure
to bring my brother
home again
when he got hungry.

# Home

Always in the half-light
come the clearest memories.
And I can see her now,
as crystal as I often did,
kneeling on the tiled
window-ledge of our family
home, with chamois in hand,

working her tired arms
in perfect rainbow arcs
across the inside of our
living room window.
To keep it clean.
To make sure it shone.
Back then, I always thought

it a gesture of welcome,
of 'Hello', of 'Come on into
our home', of 'I'll be here when you
come home from school or games'.
But now, no matter how hard
I try not to, I fear the memory,
as I know that she has always,

really, been waving goodbye.

# Full Flight

*in memory of Marylou Roddy (1930-2017)*

I stood in disbelief
as leaf after yellow leaf

fell from the birch tree
all at once

In disbelief because
each leaf falling with

a wobble and a drift
avoided the wicker

basket of lower
branches underneath

like forest birds
in full flight

Sometimes the earth
loses us like this

# Pure Theatre

*in memory of Bruce Anderson (1935–2018)*

Must feel like being
backstage before the off,

for the old man and his old boxer
shuffling out late to greet

the rose garden, the back porch,
the whole dark yard,

with not a step out of sync
for either, because when the garage

light blinks on, it's pure theatre.

# Star-Stuff

*for Anthony Alderman*

> *Nobody has the slightest idea how anything*
> *material could be conscious. Nobody even knows*
> *what it would be like to have the slightest idea how*
> *anything material could be conscious.*
> —Jerry Fodor, TLS

Paddling my way around
the early morning river
of tar that is the local

YMCA Walking Track—
little bits of mica
in its hardened body

shining in the rays
of the living sun
like so many stars—

I got taken by the thought
that even my beloved
scientists can go too far.

They've wonderfully managed
to set a few man-made
eyes up into the dark,

and now it appears that the
mystery of human existence
has been simply solved,

that we are all just
risen sparks from some
giant galactic bonfire,

the very life-blood
running through us
being a scarlet sister

to the red ore from
a dying star's core.
So there you are.

We are all just dead
stars looking back up
from Earth's watery

gutter at our starry fellows.
But didn't the Book get
this right a long time ago?

Having us formed from
the very dust of the ground?
Telling that to such dust

we will all someday return?
So what is there to unlearn?
Sometimes even my beloved

scientists unlearn their
hard-worn wisdom, ignore
occupational ignorance,

forget that what's missing
from this cosmic panorama
is way more important

than what's visibly there—
the glorious unknown
always besting the known.

We cannot exist without it,
without that great Interstellar.
Now, star-stuff we most

certainly are, but surely
it doesn't take a genius,
or some kind of simple believer,

to work out that if,
if we are made in
the image of anything

out there, it's highly unlikely
to be in the likeness
of any dead or dying star;

and it's surely still a grand
mystery to us all—that which
cannot see, now undoubtedly can.

# Forever Linked

*for Paul Anthony Custer*

The Son of Mammon, when he lifts himself up,
Will draw the unreasonable to him.

The college historian will draw a line between them
And us, redeeming his (apocryphal) ancestor's last stand.

The stall sellers, two blacks with dreadlocks, will
Peddle patriot paraphernalia to willing whites.

Young students with homemade signs—FEEL THE BERN—
Will face elderly couples angrily boasting:

*You'll feel the burn, alright, when we incinerate y'all!*
They will seek counselling, those virgin protesters.

Tempted to smile, I will understand that exposure
(For just one afternoon) to hatred can be so shocking.

Shame will surface in the town that had been hidden,
Forever linked with the Lutheran auditorium.

# 11/9

So. Here's the difference:
down at the YMCA
walking park,
the climbing tower,
generously-sponsored
by the Catawba Women's Center,
and which has always struck
me as being something
which would enter
one of my poems
as a benevolent,
giant bird-feeder,
given the leafy haven
that the park provides
for our winged friends,
now suddenly appears
as a prison yard turret.
And so begins the task
of turning it back
into a bird-feeder.

# Freedom

*for Bert & Ed and Ashley & Jen*


It was the size of an eagle,
but it must have been a hawk,
sat on top of the YMCA floodlights
that edge our local playing field,
whose baseball diamonds and soccer pitches
were all but emptied by a thunderstorm,
except for the robins and wagtails
whose field-day had suddenly dawned.

I'd juked in on the way home from the store,
doing a mercy run for bread and wine,
to dander a couple of laps of the track
in-between showers. With an eye to the sky,
I hurried round under hanging branches,
and smiled to feel that as the wind rose,
it just kind of rained again. And then,
there it was, sitting all Big Billy Badass

on its chosen perch, assuming its ownership
of the surrounding scene. But before I could
bend to its presence, robins and wagtails
shot out of the trees, in twos and threes,
taking their turns to attack it. At first,
it merely ducked its mighty head or raised
an armoured wing, but then it screeched
a long, classic screech, and flew to the next floodlight.

But the small birds hadn't finished yet.
Risking their lives, they harried it from
floodlight to floodlight around the track,
until the hawk acknowledged a measure
of defeat, gave up, and left the field.

Walking back to my car, the old dissenter's
words came back to me, and I dared to think
that even the hawk might have agreed—

*You must give freedom if you would be free.*

# High Hopes

*for MRF & CRCR*

I.

In multi-screen-lit homes,
parents fire angry aces back and forth over the taut nets
of their innocent ones.

II.

Wounded from the start,
she holds high hopes
in the locket of her heart.

# Struck

Honeyed sunlight hit
the dull grey back
of our avenue STOP sign,
changing it—
for all of a few seconds—

into a golden doubloon,
like some lost pirate's plunder
shining in shallow water,
or a celestial coin
big enough to burn a hole

in a giant's pocket.
An appropriate transiency,
I thought,
for something that struck me
as money.

# Flame

Just me and the flame
The brightest living things
Left on the evening porch

Just me and the flame
Its wind-blown self
The fabulous work of a

Frantic glass-blower, a
Mesmerising Chihuly
Flying the kite-flame

Of his instinctive art
Just me and the flame
Against the inevitable dark

# The Shadowed Path

Overhung with trees in bloom
The sun made shadows all along
One side of the walking path

And I heard a quiet voice saying
*These shadows, too, are real*
Then two large hands lifted

The shadowed path—as a child
Might lift a train track from
A playroom table top—and set it

Above the neighbouring cemetery
A gigantic installation
Of shadow-shapes in a gallery of air

# Notes & Glossary of Terms

## Notes

**The Drowning** (4)
Lines 1-3 relate to an old superstitious practice among Islandmagee fishermen.

**The Dummy Fluter** (45)
The KAI, the popular name of an infamous group of young Rathcoole Loyalists and their marching band, is an acronym for 'Kill All Irish'.

**The Gift** (38)
Spoken by a parish priest to a prospective bridegroom, this poem is based on a true story from County Derry which was recounted to me by Deirdre Coughlan. According to Robert Bell's *The Book of Ulster Surnames* (Blackstaff Press, 1988), "Browne with an *e* is more common in the south of Ireland".

**Going to the Stone** (20)
Based on the Rocking-Stone, or Giant's Cradle, which is situated on the eastern side of Brown's Bay, in the townland of Ballypriorbeg, Islandmagee. This megalith was associated with the superstitious rites of long ago: *Going to the Stone* often replaced going to church or chapel as a means of worshipping or consulting the deity; *Trial by Stone* was a method of criminal detection. The stone was said to tremble as a malefactor drew near, just as a gold chain round a judge's neck was believed to tighten upon an error being made in judgement.

**Margaret Mitchell** (6)
Inspired by a reading of the strange happenings at Knowehead, Islandmagee in 1710–1711, that led to the famous Islandmagee Witches' trial. One of the alleged witches was named Margaret Mitchell, who apparently had vowed to turn herself into a hare; *... lurker in the ditch* is a folk phrase applied to the hare; the last four lines of the poem constitute a rhyme said by young Islandmagee girls on May Day.

## The Mason's Tongue (2)

*Jah-Bul-On* is a mongrel word pertaining to a strange compound deity—the Masonic Order's 'Great Architect of the Universe'. *Jah* = Jahweh, the God of the Hebrews; *Bul* = Baal, the ancient Canaanite fertility god; *On* = Osiris, the ancient Egyptian god of the underworld.

## The Moongate Sonnets (52)

*The Moongate Sonnets* is dedicated to William Montgomery (1906–1992). I first met 'Billy' in the mid-1980s when I moved my family into a row of old terraced cottages in Mullaghboy, on the beautiful Islandmagee peninsula, on the north-eastern coast of Northern Ireland. (Ross Wilson inspired, I named the cottage 'Moongate'.) Having just lost his beloved wife, Kathleen, Billy lived on his own in the little cottage next door. Though born and bred in Belfast city, he was well-acquainted with rural Islandmagee from early childhood, and had moved there permanently following his retirement from his life-long job at Belfast's Harland & Wolff shipyard. When we met, Billy was in his late-seventies and I was in my mid-twenties, but age proved no barrier to a providential relationship. Despite the ever-present sense of loss since his passing—twenty-six years ago—I trust that the sonnets speak for themselves in regard to the evergreen essence of our friendship. As his loving family could no doubt better testify, Billy Montgomery was a genuinely humble, honourable, and honest Ulsterman.

## Rinn Seimhne Blackbird (10)

*Rinn Seimhne*, pronounced Rin Sevne or Rin Shevne, was the early Gaelic name for the Islandmagee region: Rinn meaning *point*; Seimhne, *a territory*.

## Rosebrook (37)

*Rosebrook* was the name chosen by my maternal grandparents for the home in which I was born, their timber-framed bungalow and surrounds at 30 Doagh Road, Newtownabbey, Co. Antrim (now, sadly, no more). My grandfather was Patrick 'Paddy' Hay (1909–1973); my grandmother, to whom the poem is dedicated, was Louisa Thomasina Hay, née Bingham (1917–1984).

**Shimna** (187)
The Shimna River (Irish: *Simhné*, meaning river of bulrushes) is a river in County Down, Northern Ireland. It rises on the slopes of Ott Mountain, in the beautiful Mourne Mountains, flows down through Tollymore Forest Park, and enters the Irish Sea at Newcastle, on Dundrum Bay. Famous in recent times for its Game of Thrones connection, Shimna, and the mystical forest it flows through, have long since been a true source of inspiration, comfort and sustenance for urban-based 'Troubles' folk like me; as teenagers, we would 'escape' to Tollymore as often as possible. It was our Tolkien 'Rivendell'; our Lewis 'Narnia'; our Thoreauvian retreat. A cold, playful dip in a Shimna pool not only woke you up—it *woke you up*.

**Sometimes I Think** (131)
Based on a magical day in the home of another honest Ulsterman, the quintessential 'dissenter'—the poet, critic and gallery man, John Hewitt (1907–1987). (Hewitt also figures under the moniker 'dissenter' in both "Beseech" and "Freedom".)

**The Wing** (22)
A celebration of two local characters from the past: Thomas Hill (1759–1821), one of the earliest schoolmasters in Islandmagee. Known as *The Wing* because of his slight build and mercurial disposition, he was beloved by his pupils. His remains lie within the ruined walls of the Old Church, Ballykeel, Islandmagee; William McClelland, who in 1814 was wrongly blamed for the circulation of a fanciful story regarding the capture of a mermaid at Portmuck. Many believed the report and subsequently directed their indignation at the unsuspecting McClelland.

# Glossary of Terms

| | |
|---|---|
| cassie | a country term for the well-used passage of land bordering a rural dwelling |
| fadge | potato-bread |
| flaffing | flapping |
| form | the nest or lair in which a hare crouches |
| Muck Island | *Muc* in Irish means *pig*, and the island was so named because it is shaped like a hog's back |
| Omnium Gatherum | Dog-Latin for a gathering or miscellaneous collection of all sorts of persons or things |
| pishrogues | term applied to superstitious practices and all varieties of witchcraft, fairylore, etc. |
| quidnunc | someone who is constantly asking: *What now? What's the news?*; a gossip |
| smurr | drizzle |
| soughs | sighing of wind |
| souterrain | an underground chamber, passage, etc. |
| spraightled | scrambled |
| tholing | bearing pain |
| yarrow | a composite herb, common on waste land, with flower-clusters of dull white, often varying to pink or crimson |

# Index of Titles

Photograph by Alan Dehmer

Cover photographer John Rosenthal is a recipient of a North Carolina Visual Art Fellowship for his photographs of New Orleans' Lower Ninth Ward. His work has been exhibited throughout the North and Southeast, and his one-person shows include exhibits at The National Humanities Center, New Orleans African-American Museum, Boston's Panopticon Gallery, The National Academy of Sciences in Washington D.C., and North Carolina State University's Gregg Museum. His work can be found in various collections including The North Carolina Museum of Art, the Gregg Museum of Art and Design, the Cassilhaus Collection, and the Collection of R. J. Reynolds. His books include *Regarding Manhattan, After: The Silence of the Lower 9th Ward* and *Quartet: Four North Carolina Photographers*.

Photograph by Jon Eckard

Adrian Rice is from north Belfast, Northern Ireland. He was brought up in the Rathcoole Housing Estate, and attended Ballyclare High School. He graduated from the University of Ulster with a BA in English & Politics, and MPhil in Anglo-Irish Literature, writing his thesis on the doctor-poet who coined the phrase "the Emerald Isle", Dr. William Drennan (1754–1820). His first sequence of poems appeared in *Muck Island* (Moongate Publications, 1990), a collaboration with leading Irish artist, Ross Wilson. Copies of this limited edition box-set are housed in the collections of The Tate Gallery, and The Boston Museum of Fine Arts. In 1997, Rice received the Sir James Kilfedder Memorial Bursary for Emerging Artists. In autumn 1999, as recipient of the US/Ireland Exchange Bursary, he was Poet-in-Residence at Lenoir-Rhyne College, Hickory, NC. His first full poetry collection—*The Mason's Tongue* (Abbey Press, 1999)—was shortlisted for the Christopher Ewart-Biggs Memorial Literary Prize, nominated for the Irish Times Prize for Poetry, and translated into Hungarian by Thomas Kabdebo (*A Komuves Nyelve*, epl/ ediotio plurilingua, 2005). In 2002, he co-edited a major Irish anthology entitled, *A Conversation Piece: Poetry and Art* (The Ulster Museum in association with Abbey Press). His poems and reviews have been broadcast internationally on radio and television, and have been published in several international magazines and journals. Selections of his poetry and prose have appeared in both *The Belfast Anthology* and *The Ulster Anthology* (Ed., Patricia Craig, Blackstaff Press, 1999 & 2006) and in *Magnetic North: The Emerging Poets* (Ed., John Brown, Lagan Press, 2006). A chapbook, *Hickory Haiku*, was published in 2010 by Finishing Line Press, Kentucky. Rice returned to Lenoir-Rhyne College as Visiting Writer-in-Residence for 2005. Since then, Adrian and his wife Molly, and young son, Micah, have settled in Hickory, from where he commutes to Boone for Doctoral studies at Appalachian State University. During his time in Hickory, Adrian has taught English and Creative Writing at several local colleges, including Lenoir-Rhyne University, and Catawba Valley Community College, and has also taught at ASU for the Reading program. He currently teaches in ASU's First Year Seminar Program. He has also teamed up with Hickory-based and fellow Belfastman, musician/songwriter Alan Mearns, to form 'The Belfast Boys', a dynamic Irish Traditional Music duo. Their debut album, *Songs For Crying Out Loud*, regularly airs across the Carolinas. Adrian's previous two books, *The Clock Flower* (2013), and *Hickory Station* (2015) are both published by Press 53.